Early Praise for *Trauma-Proofing Your Kids*

"Peter Levine and Maggie Kline have done an outstanding job of helping parents, and everyone else, to understand the different kinds of trauma children may face. I have done a lot of work in therapy around my own traumatic childhood event and was able to try out many of the easy-to-follow exercises they provide. I truly felt a relief and peacefulness that I had never felt before. I treasure this book and hope you will too."

> – *Violet Oaklander, PhD, author of* Windows to Our Children:
> A Gestalt Therapy Approach to Children and Adolescents *and*
> Hidden Treasure: A Map to the Child's Inner Self

"If you've ever wondered how to help children navigate the rough and tumble vicissitudes of life, this book is a godsend."

> – *Sandra Blakeslee, co-author of* The Body Has a Mind of Its Own

"This book is a must for every parent, teacher, coach and scout leader. It helps us to understand the stages of childhood development and supports parents in dealing with each stage more appropriately and sensitively. It is a pioneering work, a pioneering insight and a pioneering triumph. It is visionary common sense, pure and simple."

> – *From the foreword by Mira Rothenberg*

"*Trauma-Proofing Your Kids* is an important tool to help parents and *all* adults deal with children that have experienced trauma. Understanding that trauma is a part of life should signal all of us to prepare ourselves for the inevitable."

> – *Ron Scruggs, athletic coach, parent and grandparent*

Praise for *Trauma Through A Child's Eyes*

"A truly remarkable book that captures the essence of what it is to be a traumatized child, while simultaneously helping us understand, appreciate and facilitate their natural capacity to heal. Written with a deep sense of compassion and wisdom, this book offers clear insight to those who care for and about children."

> – *John Stewart, PhD, author of* Beyond Time Out; *clinical director, MSE/MHC; Child Psychiatry Fellowship Faculty, Maine Medical Center; consultant to public schools*

"Some books are said, in their originality, to 'break the mold.' *Trauma Through A Child's Eyes* goes further: it creates its own mold in a way that everyone concerned with the health and happiness of children will be grateful for."

> – *Gabor Mate, MD, author of* Hold Onto Your Kids: Why Parents Need to Matter More than Peers

"This is the most valuable method I have found to help children reclaim their vitality, alleviate symptoms and develop resiliency to future threats. I only wish I had possessed these skills when the American Red Cross assigned me to the Pentagon Special Response Team in Washington, DC, after 9/11."

> – *Lisa R. LaDue, MSW, LISW, senior advisor (co-founder and former director), National Mass Fatalities Institute, University of Iowa*

"*Trauma Through A Child's Eyes* is one of the most valuable gifts one can give to friends, colleagues, parents, relations, and all other people who care about children; it is our choice for the book of the year."

> – *The International Society for the Scientific Prevention of Violence*

"What could be more empowering than teaching our children how to unlock their innate resiliency, release trauma and return to calm? I am thankful to the authors for the lives of the children they touch by their good work."

> – *Pepper Black, program director, Office of Student Development, University of California, Berkeley*

TRAUMA-PROOFING YOUR KIDS

A Parents' Guide for Instilling Confidence, Joy and Resilience

PETER A. LEVINE, PhD

MAGGIE KLINE, MS, MFT
(Marriage & Family Therapist)
and School Psychologist

North Atlantic Books
Berkeley, California

ERGOS Institute Press
Lyons, Colorado

Published by

North Atlantic Books   and   ERGOS Institute Press
Huichin, unceded Ohlone land   P.O. Box 110
aka Berkeley, California   Lyons, Colorado 80540

Cover photo © iStockphoto.com/Daniela Andreea Spyropoulos
Cover and book design © Ayelet Maida, A/M Studios
Printed in the United States of America

Trauma-Proofing Your Kids: A Parents' Guide for Instilling Confidence, Joy and Resilience is sponsored and published by North Atlantic Books, an educational nonprofit based in the unceded Ohlone land Huichin (aka Berkeley, CA) that collaborates with partners to develop cross-cultural perspectives; nurture holistic views of art, science, the humanities, and healing; and seed personal and global transformation by publishing work on the relationship of body, spirit, and nature.

North Atlantic Books' publications are distributed to the US trade and internationally by Penguin Random House Publishers Services. For further information, visit our website at www.northatlanticbooks.com.

Library of Congress Cataloging-in-Publication Data

Levine, Peter A.
   Trauma-proofing your kids : a parents' guide for instilling confidence, joy, and resilience / by Peter A. Levine & Maggie Kline.
      p. cm.
   Summary: "This book assists parents and other lay caregivers in the prevention and healing of trauma by serving as a practical guide to "stress-busting" and building resilience in kids so they can easily cope with our fast-changing world of mishaps, increasing pressures and turbulence"—Provided by publisher.
   Includes bibliographical references
   ISBN 978-1-55643-699-4
1. Psychic trauma in children—Prevention—Popular works. 2. Post-traumatic stress disorder in children—Prevention—Popular works. 3. Resilience (Personality trait) in children. I. Kline, Maggie. II. Title.
   RJ506.P55L48 2008
618.92'8521—dc22   2007042471

10 11 12 13 14 15 KPC 26 25 24 23 22 21

Contents

Dedication and Acknowledgments

From Peter A. Levine

Trauma-Proofing Your Kids is dedicated to my godchildren, Jacob, Jada and Ossian. Participation in your lives, from birth to childhood, and then through adolescence into young adulthood, has been a gift beyond all measures. You and the many other infants, babies, toddlers, children and teenagers I have encountered along the way have taught me more about healing than all of the academic texts in the world. This book is dedicated to you, with the deepest appreciation and with the passionate hope that what I have learned from you can be shared with all the mommies and daddies so that they can better guide their kids through the tribulations, defeats and ultimate triumphs of life. And enduring thankfulness to all the children of the world; you are our hope for the future.

I also have a deep appreciation for my students (many of whom are now colleagues). To Ana DoValle, OT, I appreciate her sensitive perceptions in work with traumatized infants. I thank Juliana DoValle (now a young woman on her way to a brilliant acting and writing career), who at age eleven drew the illustrations that appear in these pages. I thank Lorin Hager, who helped refine the verses. And finally, enormous gratitude goes to Maggie Kline, my most talented and creative colleague and fellow mischief-maker. I am indebted, more than words can express, for her support, commitment, dedication and her plain hard work.

From Maggie Kline

I dedicate this book to my son Jake, who has taught me so much about what kids need to be confident, joyful and resilient. I am grateful for his generous spirit, support and tenacity in facing life's challenges.

I wish to express heartfelt appreciation to all the children and teens that I have worked and played with over the years, both in inner-city schools and private practice. I am grateful for their courage, openness, candor and spontaneity, for they have taught me to listen, follow their lead and trust in their innate capacity to heal, even from the most egregious wounds. Most of all, I wish to thank Peter Levine, who originated and developed Somatic Experiencing® to prevent and heal trauma. His mentorship, wisdom, passion, inspiration and love have changed both my personal and professional life profoundly and forever. His vision for the future of the world's children is more than just a vision—it is a clear and simple path that parents can take step-by-step to alleviate unnecessary suffering. For his big-hearted nature and care for all children, I am most grateful.

Foreword

A Tale for Our Times

Once upon a time—a long, long time ago—there was a beautiful kingdom.

The King that ruled this kingdom was a very wise and kind person, but an unhappy one. The King had a daughter whom he loved very much; a smart and beautiful eight-year-old child. But this little girl refused to leave the palace, never going outside and crying desperately whenever she saw a dog or even heard a bark.

The King then gave out an edict: "No dogs in the kingdom." So all the dogs were banished. But that did not help his daughter's phobia, and besides, the other children were greatly saddened by this order. The Princess still would not leave the palace. The King then wrote another proclamation: "Anyone who can get my daughter to leave the house can have half of my kingdom."

In the countryside lived an old wizard and a wise woman: Peter Levine and his dear friend Maggie Kline. They announced that they could remedy the situation. The King agreed. Peter and Maggie came to the palace and explained that the child suffered from trauma (having been bitten by a dog when she was four years old). Using the wisdom outlined in this book, they proceeded to heal the child of her affliction. To the King's surprise and joy, the Princess started going outside the palace and soon requested a puppy dog.

The kingdom was jubilant. All the dogs returned and the children were able to play with their beloved companions again. No one loved her dog more than the Princess. "Now," said the King to Peter and Maggie, "half of my kingdom is yours."

"We don't want half of your kingdom," they replied. "We have one inside of ourselves. But we do want to talk to all of the parents in your country so that we can teach them how to prevent and overcome their children's traumas. The King was amazed and delighted. "Of course! Your wish will be fulfilled immediately." And so it was.

It was a happy nation after that. It was a nation where bullies, fighting and fear were at a minimum, and kids were free to learn and to love learning. It was a nation where even war and sexual attacks were eliminated into the second, third and fourth generations.

Peter Levine and Maggie Kline are most remarkable human beings. *Trauma-Proofing Your Kids* conveys their precious gifts with simple explanations, inspired experiential exercises and rich examples taken from children they have known and helped. Their combined knowledge and empathy for children in all stages of development is astonishing. Not only do they have this exquisite understanding of children, but of their parents too. Peter and Maggie teach us how to understand and respect our children's pain, their joy and their terror, and thus how to produce a happier, more confident and resilient generation of kids, adolescents and adults. This book is a must for every parent, teacher, coach and scout leader. It helps us to understand the stages of childhood development and supports parents in dealing with each stage more appropriately and sensitively. It is a pioneering work, a pioneering insight and a pioneering triumph. It is visionary common sense, pure and simple.

– Mira Rothenberg
Author of Children with Emerald Eyes:
Stories of Extraordinary Boys and Girls *and
co-founder and director emeritus of the Blue
Berry Treatment Centers, Brooklyn, New York*

CHAPTER I

Trauma Is a Fact of Life

The bad news is that trauma is a fact of life. The good news is that so is resilience. Simply stated, resilience is the capacity we all possess to rebound from stress and feelings of fear, helplessness and overwhelm. The analogy sometimes given for resilience is that of a metal spring, such as a "Slinky." If you pull it apart, the coil naturally rebounds to its original size and shape. Of course, if you stretch this spring too many times (or exert too much force), it will eventually lose its elasticity.

People (especially young people), however, need not lose their resilience through wear and tear. On the contrary, we have the capacity to actually build and increase our resilience as we encounter the stresses and strains of life. Resilient children tend to be courageous. This doesn't mean that they are attracted to dangerous situations, but rather that they are *open* and *curious* as they explore their world with gusto and exuberance. And, in their explorations, they inevitably have their share of rumbles and tumbles, collisions and conflicts.

When resilient kids meet these forces of nature, they are open rather than shut down. Openness, indeed, is the characteristic that most typifies resilient kids. They are open to other children and enjoy sharing with them. At the same time, they are able to set boundaries of their own personal space and their possessions. They are in touch with their feelings, expressing and communicating them in age-appropriate ways. And, most of all, when bad things happen, they have a wondrous capacity (when supported) to breeze through them. They are the happy, lively children we wish we were.

Their biggest challenges occur from events that could be potentially traumatic. Let's delve into what types of life's circumstances might cause such overwhelming reactions in our kids.

Trauma can result from events that are clearly extraordinary such as violence and molestation, but it can also result from everyday "ordinary" events. In fact, common occurrences such as accidents, falls, medical procedures and divorce can cause children to withdraw, lose confidence, or develop anxiety and phobias. Traumatized children may also display behavioral problems including aggression, hyperactivity and, as they grow older, addictions of various sorts. The good news is that with the guidance of attuned parents and other caregivers who are willing to learn the necessary skills, children at risk can be identified and spared from being scarred for life, regardless of how devastating the events might be or seem.

Parents are, at times, conflicted between protecting their children and permitting them to take the risks that build confidence and competence. It's a tricky balancing act because as they master their world, children can also be traumatized when the unexpected inevitably happens. As much as you may try to "child-proof" your home, ultimately children—driven by their curiosity—will explore and get hurt. That *is* how they learn and they *will* have their share of falls, burns, electrical shocks, animal bites and other encounters with the non-forgiving forces of nature. No matter how hard we try, we cannot close our children off in an impenetrable (and inescapable) bubble of safety.

Our children are frequently exposed to *potentially* traumatic events. But parents need not despair. It is possible to minimize the effects of the "ordinary" situations mentioned above, as well as those from extraordinary events such as natural and man-made disasters, including violence, war, terrorism and molestation.

Are we being ridiculous by proposing that adults can "trauma-proof" kids? We don't believe so. *Remember, although pain can't be avoided ... trauma is a fact of life ... but so is resilience, the capacity to spring back.*

In this book you will learn practical tools to maximize your child's resilience so that their equilibrium can be restored when they are stressed to their breaking point. Armed with this "recipe for resilience," parents and other responsible adults can help to trauma-proof their kids while also generally increasing their tolerance to everyday stress. In this way they can truly become stronger, more caring, joyful and compassionate human beings.

The word "trauma" pops up in the headlines of magazines and newspapers regularly. Popular TV shows such as *The Oprah Winfrey Show* bring understanding to millions of viewers regarding trauma's gripping effect on body and soul. Trauma's devastating impact on children's emotional and physical well-being, mental development and behavior is finally getting the recognition it deserves. Since September 11, 2001, there has been an information blitz on how to cope with catastrophe.

Despite this focus, however, precious little has been written regarding the common causes or the prevention and the non-drug treatment of trauma. Focus instead has been on the diagnosis and the medication of its various symptoms. "Trauma is perhaps the most avoided, ignored, belittled, denied, misunderstood, and untreated cause of human suffering."[1] Fortunately, you—the parents, aunts, uncles and grandparents who nurture and protect children—are in a position to prevent, or at least mitigate, the damaging effects of trauma.

In order to do the most good for the children in your care, first you need to recognize the roots of trauma. Next, we take a closer look at trauma—its myths and realities. In this way you will understand what may cause a child to remain overwhelmed even though the actual danger has passed.

This book will teach you how to help children notice and move through painful sensations and feelings without undue distress. Your new knowledge will help take the fear out of the experience of the involuntary reactions and emotions that allow children to rebound from trauma as well as other difficult feelings. Many real-life examples are included to illustrate how you can support children in recovering from overwhelming experiences. You will learn to recognize the signs of trauma while acquiring simple skills to alleviate or prevent trauma symptoms after a frightening mishap or stressful life event. While these basic principles are meant to be "emotional first aid" applied by conscientious caregivers, there are situations, of course, when professional counseling is highly recommended. We will help you to know when this might be necessary.

Real-Life Examples of Children We Have Known

By taking a peek into the worlds of five different children, you will have a better sense of the scope of trauma that can occur at any age. One or two of the situations described may even remind you of your own kids! After you read the dilemmas of the youngsters below, you will discover what caused their behavior.

Lisa cries hysterically every time the family prepares to get into the car.

Carlos, a painfully shy fifteen-year-old, is chronically truant. "I don't want to feel scared all the time anymore," he says. "All I want is to feel normal."

Sarah reports dutifully to her second-grade class on time every morning; invariably, by 11 a.m., she is in the nurse's office complaining of a stomachache, although no medical reason can be found for her chronic symptoms.

Curtis, a popular, good-natured middle school student, tells his mother that he feels like kicking someone—anyone! He has no idea where this urge is coming from. Two weeks later he starts behaving aggressively, bullying his little brother.

The parents of three-year-old Kevin are concerned about his "hyperactivity" and "autistic-like" play when he feels stressed. He repeatedly lies on the floor and stiffens his body, pretending he is dying and slowly coming back to life, saying, "Save me . . . save me!"

What do these youngsters have in common? How did their symptoms originate? Will their symptoms disappear or grow worse over time? To answer these questions, let's take a look at where their troubles began.

We'll start with Lisa, the hysterical crier. When she was three years old, she had been strapped into her car seat when the family's van was rear-ended. There were no physical injuries to her or her mom, who was driving. In fact, the car was barely scratched and the accident was considered a minor "fender bender." Little Lisa's crying was not associated with the accident because it took several weeks before the numbing impact of the collision wore off. Her initial symptoms (shortly after the accident) were unusually quiet behavior coupled with a poor appetite. Her parents thought she was "over it" when her appetite returned. Instead her symptoms changed to fearful tears whenever she came near the family van.

While Lisa experienced a one-time episode, Carlos' symptoms developed over time. He had been physically intimidated for more than five years by an emotionally disturbed teenaged stepbrother. No one intervened. His parents considered it "normal" sibling rivalry. They didn't have a clue that Carlos was terrified of his brother because he locked his secret deep inside, fearful that his parents would be furious with him for not being empathetic to his brother's disability. He had tried to express his dread to his mother but his feelings were dismissed; he was, instead, asked to be more tolerant.

No one except Carlos' older sister, who was in distress herself due to the family dynamics, saw his pain or predicament.

Meanwhile, Carlos fantasized night and day about being a professional wrestler, but he had barely enough strength or confidence to get out of bed to come to school, let alone become part of a high school sports team. It wasn't until Carlos revealed a plan for suicide at school that his parents finally recognized the heavy emotional toll that the repeated harassment was having on their son.

The next youngster mentioned above was Sarah, who had been very excited about starting second grade. After a fun shopping spree with mom to pick out brand-new clothes for school, she was told, abruptly and unexpectedly, that her parents were getting divorced and her father would be moving out in two weeks! Her joy for school became paired with panic and sadness. The aliveness in her tummy changed into tight twisted knots. No wonder she was the nurse's most frequent visitor!

While waiting for the school bus one morning, Curtis witnessed a drive-by shooting that left the victim dead on the sidewalk. He was with a small group of classmates at the bus stop, and all received some counseling when they arrived at school. Curtis, however, continued to look disturbed and agitated as the days passed.

The last youngster described was Kevin. He had been delivered by emergency cesarean and had a lifesaving surgery within twenty-four hours of his birth. He was born with anomalies requiring immediate intestinal and rectal repair. Often, medical and surgical procedures are required and do make life possible. Amidst the relief and celebration of a saved life, it is easy to overlook the reality that these same procedures can inflict trauma that may leave emotional and behavioral effects long after the surgical wounds have healed.

Except for the shooting witnessed by Curtis and the major surgery performed on Kevin at birth, the situations above are not extraordinary; in fact, they happen to many children. Although each "event" was very different, what these youngsters have in common is that each experienced feelings of overwhelm and helplessness. Each youngster was traumatized by what happened and *how* they experienced what happened. How do we know? The answer is quite simple. Each child carried on in life, some way, as if the event were still happening. They were "stuck" in time, as their bodies responded to an alarm that was set at the traumatic moment. Although these children may not remember the event (or their parents may not connect their symptoms to it), their play, behavior and physical complaints reveal their struggle to cope with the new and frightening feelings they have inside.

The above examples demonstrate the breadth and depth of common situations that can be overwhelming to children. Throughout this book, examples and first-aid suggestions will be given on how to deal with a variety of situations, both ordinary and extraordinary, at various ages and stages of a child's life.

Trauma Is Not Only in the Event

Trauma happens when an intense experience stuns a child like a bolt out of the blue; it overwhelms the child, leaving him altered and disconnected from his body, mind and spirit. Any coping mechanisms the child may have had are undermined, and he feels utterly helpless. It is as if his legs are knocked out from under him. Trauma can also be the result of ongoing fear and nervous tension. Long-term stress responses wear down a child, causing an erosion of health, vitality and confidence. This was clearly the case with Carlos and his bully brother.

Trauma is the antithesis of empowerment. Vulnerability to trauma differs from child to child depending on a variety of factors, especially age, quality of early bonding, trauma history and genetic predisposition. The younger the child, the more likely she is to be overwhelmed by common occurrences that might not affect an older child or adult. It has been commonly believed that the severity of traumatic symptoms is equivalent to the severity of the event. While the magnitude of the stressor is clearly an important factor, it does not define trauma. Here the child's capacity for resilience is paramount. In addition, "trauma resides not in the event itself; but rather [its effect] in the nervous system."[2] The basis of "single-event" trauma (as contrasted to ongoing neglect and abuse) is primarily *physiological* rather than psychological.

What we mean by "physiological" is that there is no time to think when facing threat; therefore our primary responses are instinctual. Our brain's main function is survival! We are wired for it. At the root of a traumatic reaction is our 280-million-year heritage—a heritage that resides in the oldest and deepest structures of the brain. When these primitive parts of the brain perceive danger, they automatically activate an extraordinary amount of energy—like the adrenaline rush that allows a mother to lift an auto to pull her trapped child to safety. We personally know a woman whose arm was trapped under the tire of a truck as an eight-year-old girl. Rescue workers were unsuccessful in helping her until they were able to get her father to the scene. With his powerful, protective, bear-like surge of energy, he was able to pull her out.

This fathomless survival energy that we all share elicits a pounding heart along with more than twenty other physiological responses designed to prepare us to defend and protect ourselves and our loved ones. These rapid involuntary shifts include the redirection of blood flow away from the digestive and skin organs and into the large motor muscles of flight, along with fast and shallow respiration and a decrease in the normal output of saliva. Pupils dilate to increase the ability of the eyes to take in more information. Blood-clotting ability increases, while verbal ability decreases. Muscles become highly excited, often causing our child to tremble. Alternatively, when faced with mortal threat or prolonged stress, certain muscles may collapse in fear as the body shuts down in an overwhelmed state.

Fear of Our Own Reactions

When a child or adult is uncomfortable with what is happening inside them (their inner sensations and feelings), the very responses that are meant to give a physical advantage can become downright frightening. This is especially true when, due to size, age or other vulnerabilities, one is either unable to move or it would be disadvantageous to do so. For example, an infant or young child doesn't have the option to run and escape from a source of danger or threat. However, an older child or an adult, who ordinarily could run, may also need to keep very still, such as in the case of surgery, rape or molestation. There is no conscious choice. We are biologically programmed to freeze (or go limp) when flight or fight is either impossible or perceived to be impossible. Freeze and collapse are the last-ditch, "default" responses to an inescapable threat, even if that threat is a microbe in our blood. Infants and children, because of their limited capacity to defend themselves, are particularly susceptible to freezing and therefore are vulnerable to being traumatized. This is why the adult's skill is so crucial in providing emotional first aid to a frightened youngster. Parental support can slowly move a child out of acute stress to empowerment and even joy.

What must be understood about the freeze response is that although the body *looks* inert, those physiological mechanisms that prepare the body to escape may still be on "full charge." Muscles that were poised for action at the time of threat are thrown into a state of immobility or "shock." When in shock the skin is pale and the eyes vacant. Breathing is shallow and rapid, or just shallow. The sense of time is distorted. Underlying this situation of helplessness, however, there is an enormous vital energy. This energy lies in wait to finish whatever action had been initiated. In addition, very young children tend to bypass active responses, becoming motionless instead. Later, even though the danger is over, a simple reminder can send the exact same alarm signals racing once again through the body until it shuts down. When this happens we may see the child becoming sullen, depressed, whiney, clingy and withdrawn.

Whether your child is still fully charged or has shut down, your guidance is imperative to alleviate their traumatic stress response and to build up their resilience. Furthermore, young children generally protect themselves not by running away, but by running toward the protective adult. Hence, to help the child resolve a trauma, there must be a safe adult to support them. The parent who has the skills of emotional first aid can help them literally "shake things off" and breathe freely again.

How does the outpouring of survival energy and multiple changes in physiology affect our kids over time? The answer to this question is an important one in understanding the consequences of trauma. This depends on what happens during and after the threat. The catch is that to avoid being traumatized, the excess energy mobilized to defend us must be "used up." When the energy is not fully discharged, it does not simply go away; instead it remains as a kind of "body memory" creating the potential for repeated traumatic symptoms.

The younger the child, the fewer resources she has to protect herself. For example, a preschool or primary-school child is unable to escape from or fight a vicious dog, while infants are unable even to keep themselves warm. For these reasons the protection of respectful adults who perceive and meet children's needs for security, warmth and tranquility (and respect for their boundaries) is of paramount importance in preventing trauma. Additionally, adults often can provide comfort and safety by introducing a stuffed toy animal, doll, angel or even a fantasy character that can act as a surrogate friend. These objects can be especially consoling when children must be temporarily separated from their parents, and as sleeping aids when they are alone in their room at night.

Resources such as these may seem silly for an adult but may prove vital to the young child in preventing overwhelm.

Adults who received this type of secure connection when frightened as children may call the above information "common sense." This implies that children's needs are commonly noticed and attended to. Historically, however, the needs of children have been disgracefully minimized, if not overlooked entirely. Developmental psychiatrist Daniel Siegel, author of the acclaimed book *The Developing Mind,* provides a synthesis of the neurobiological research underscoring exactly how crucial the safety and containment provided by adults is to infants and children. The early brain develops its intelligence, emotional resilience and ability to self-regulate (restore equilibrium) by the anatomical-neuronal "shaping" and "pruning" that takes place within the face-to-face relationship between child and caregiver. When traumatic events occur, the imprinting of neurological patterns is dramatically heightened. Thus when adults learn and practice the simple emotional first aid tools we offer, they are also making a pivotal contribution to healthy brain development and behavior in their children.

The Recipe for Trauma

The likelihood of developing traumatic symptoms is related to the level of shutdown as well as to the residual survival energy that was originally mobilized to fight or flee. This self-protective process has now gone haywire. Children need consistent, patient support to release this highly charged state and return to healthy, flexible functioning. The myth can be laid to rest that babies and toddlers "are too young to be affected" by adverse events or that "it won't matter because they won't remember." What was not so obvious becomes apparent as we learn that prenatal infants, newborns and very young children are the most at risk to stress and trauma due to their undeveloped nervous, muscular and perceptual systems. This vulnerability also applies to older children who have limited mobility because of permanent or temporary disabilities, such as having a splint, brace or cast due to an orthopedic injury or correction. Included in this category are children less able-bodied due to cerebral palsy, congenital deformities or developmental delays.

The Reason Our Bodies Don't Forget: What Brain Research Has Taught Us

Why is it that once the threat is over we are not free of it? Why are we left with anxiety and vivid memories that alter us forever if we don't get the help that we need?

The highly regarded neurologist Antonio Damasio, author of *Descartes' Error* and *The Feeling of What Happens*, discovered that emotions literally have an anatomical mapping in the brain necessary for survival.[3] That is to say, the emotion of fear has a very specific neural circuitry etched in the brain corresponding to specific physical sensations from various parts of the body. When something we see, hear, smell or taste evokes similar body sensations to a previous threat, the emotions of fear and helplessness are again evoked, mimicking what happened when the initial danger was present. Originally, the experience of fear served an important purpose. It helped the body to organize a "flee or freeze" plan to remove us from peril quickly. However, the trigger now produces a similar fear even though there is no conscious memory of its origin (just the identical physical response). The heart rate escalates rapidly or drops precipitously, sweat is produced, and the anguish occurs because the body is totally re-engaged, mistaking the body's responses for the original threat as if it were actually happening in present time. But what parents are more likely to observe are seemingly inexplicable behaviors and emotions.

The Recipe for Resilience

As we explained earlier in this chapter, whether a child remains distressed or bounces back with resilience depends on what happens during and/or after the threat. You have learned that to avoid being traumatized, the excess energy that your child mobilized in a failed attempt to protect or defend himself *must* be accessed and then "used up." When this "emergency" energy is not fully engaged and discharged, it does not simply go away. Instead, it is capable of causing all sorts of troublesome symptoms, as you shall see shortly with "Henry." You will also see how Henry's aversion for and his avoidance of certain foods and noises soon disappeared as he "used up" his anxious energy to joyfully rebound with the support of his parents. And, the skills that Henry's parents utilized are the same skills that you will be learning throughout this book to help your child when she is apprehensive, stressed or outright terrified after a frightening challenge.

HENRY

Four-year-old Henry's mother became concerned when he refused to eat his (previously) favorite foods: peanut butter and jelly with a glass of milk. When his mother placed them in front of Henry, he would get agitated, stiffen and push them away. Even more disturbing was the fact that he would start shaking and crying whenever the family dog barked. It never occurred to her that this "pickiness" and fearfulness of the barking were directly related to an "ordinary" incident that had occurred almost a year before, when Henry was still using a high chair.

Sitting in his high chair, devouring his favorite foods—peanut butter, jelly and milk—he had proudly held out his half-empty glass for his mother to fill. As things like this happen, Henry lost his grip and the glass fell to the ground with a crash. This startled the dog, causing it to jump backward, knocking over the high chair. Henry hit his head on the floor and lay there, gasping, unable to catch his breath. Mother screamed and the dog started barking loudly. From his mother's perspective Henry's food aversion and apparent fear of the dog made no sense. However, from the vantage of trauma, the simple association of having milk and peanut butter right before the fall and the wild barking of his dog, in a Pavlovian response, conditioned his fear and aversion to his previously favorite foods.

Once Henry had "practiced" controlled falling onto pillows (with the suggestions detailed later in this book), he learned to relax his previously stiffened muscles as he gradually surrendered to gravity. Before this, he "simply" would not eat those foods and had trouble sleeping when dogs barked in the neighborhood. Fortunately, after a couple of play sessions this little boy was once again devouring his favorite foods and barking back at the dog in playful glee. In other words, Henry got to use up the energy that was bound up in his defenses against falling during these safe "tumbling sessions." As he gained mastery of his balance—with the help and safety of his parents—Henry's fear was transformed into delight.

CHAPTER II

Building Resilience
by Building Sensory Awareness Skills
through Practice, Practice
and More Practice

In order to build your child's capacity to rebound after overwhelming situations you will first need to learn and practice several skills. This chapter provides a variety of exercises that will enable you and your child to discover the rich sensory landscape that exists within the body. Likely, they will be fun and enlivening for you and your family. Guidance will also be given that helps parents and children acquire a *new* vocabulary for this *new* terrain. The language of sensation is communicated from the deep recesses of the brain—what we shall call the "body-brain." You will become adept at recognizing these spontaneous internal signals and promptings that arise from this instinctual part of you. Becoming proficient in these skills lessens the rift between conscious and unconscious bodily processes. This *experiential* knowledge of sensations will not only give you the tools to assist your overwhelmed child; it has the side benefit of helping you, the parents, avoid becoming distraught as well. In this chapter you will learn how to attune to your child's needs and rhythms, with a guide to hone your observation skills through looking, listening and resonating with him.

Giving Appropriate Support to an Overwhelmed Child

In order to prevent or minimize trauma and alleviate stress, it is important to make sure that *you're* not overwrought by your child's mishap. It goes without saying that this is not always easy! However, children, by their nature, are both fragile *and* resilient. It may be comforting to know that with the proper support, they are usually able to rebound from stressful events. In fact, as they begin to triumph over life's shocks and losses, kids grow into more competent, resilient and vibrant beings. Because the capacity to heal is *innate,* your role as an adult is simple: it is to help youngsters access this capacity. Your task is similar in many ways to the function of a band-aid or a splint. The band-aid or splint doesn't heal the wound but protects and supports the body as it restores itself. The suggestions, exercises and step-by-step guidelines provided here are meant to enable you to be a good "band-aid" for your child.

The importance of the adult's composure cannot be overemphasized. Calm is essential! When a child has been hurt or frightened, it is normal for the adult to feel somewhat shocked and scared, too. Because of your own fears and protective instincts, it is not uncommon to respond initially with fear and anger. However, this can further frighten your child. The goal is to minimize—not to compound—the feelings of fright, shame, embarrassment and guilt your child may already be experiencing. The best antidote is to tend to your own reactions *first.* Allow time for your own bodily responses to settle rather than scolding or running anxiously toward your child, unless she is actually in danger. Experiences with our adult clients in therapy confirm that often the most frightening part of an incident experienced as a child was their parents' horror reaction! Children "read" the facial expression of their caregivers as a barometer of how serious the danger or injury is.

Simple Steps to Build Resilience

The way to develop a calm adult presence is through practice. The experiential exercises provided will increase your ability to restore equilibrium, quickly and naturally, so you are more likely to experience grace under pressure. Once your body learns that "what goes up (charge/excitation/fear) *can* come down (discharge/

relaxation/security)," you are on the way to a more resilient nervous system, one that can weather the ups and downs of life. You will become more like the tall bamboo or wispy willow that bends, sometimes to the ground, but does not break even during a monsoon! When your body "gets it," you become contagious—in a good way. Through body language, facial expression and tone of voice, your own nervous system communicates directly with your child's nervous system. This is how we *truly* connect with our kids! It's not our words that have the greatest impact; it's the non-verbal cues that create the feelings of safety and trust. Before you can attune to your child's sensations, rhythms and emotions, you must first learn to attune to your own. Then your calm can become their calm.

The first step in this attunement process is to understand the importance of experiencing both comfortable and uncomfortable sensations while learning to tolerate and, little by little, befriend them. It is essential in becoming resilient. This deeper experience of ourselves, often neglected, shapes our core being. It is from our own breath and belly that we form our sense of self and help our children to sense theirs.

At first, when exploring physical sensations, it may be difficult to stay focused on them. But each time we do it becomes a bit easier. It is important to be able to tolerate displeasure long enough for the sensation to change, as it inevitably will. It is equally important to be able to experience increased pleasure and joy. As you practice, your body is able to hold (and "contain") more sensation and emotion without getting stressed and making you feel like freaking out. Once adults feel more "at home" with their feelings and sensations, they naturally become models to their kids of how best to embody emotions.

Developing a Calming Presence

If being a balanced, centered adult presence in an emergency is not your normal mode, no need to despair. Given the modern stresses of juggling family and career responsibilities—not to mention personal problems and any of your own unresolved traumas—how on earth is a parent or other caregiver supposed to be calm and resilient? This is *especially* tricky in the case of a crisis, such as watching a toddler's first acrobatic plunge down the stairs or through a plate-glass window!

In order for you to become more resilient and effective—not only in handling domestic disasters, but with parenting in general—it's vital that you gain an experiential sense of how your own instincts operate when in danger or under stress. So how does one go about learning to be a bastion of cool when the baby's crying and your toddler just poked himself in the eye with a stick? Let's get started by learning about what goes on inside your "body-brain" (and your child's) when you are frightened or unduly stressed.

The Body-Brain Connection

Humans have a triune brain (three distinctive brains functioning together as one mind). Simply put, this means that there are three parts that, ideally, work in harmony. The neocortical or newest part of the brain is responsible for complex thinking skills such as problem-solving, planning and perception, as well as social functioning. The mammalian (midbrain) or limbic system is also referred to as the "emotional brain"[1] because it processes memories and feelings. The reptilian or "lower" brain is responsible for survival through the myriad functions that accompany the regulatory mechanisms of basic existence, such as heart rate and respiration. These include the workings of our nervous system that interact with our sensory and motor systems to move us quickly out of danger. These primitive brain parts form the basic body-brain connection.

Each region of our triune brain has very specialized functions, and each speaks its own "language." The thinking brain speaks with words, while the emotional brain uses the language of feelings, such as anger, sorrow, joy, disgust and fear. Young children easily learn to label the emotions: mad, sad, glad, scared and "grossed-out" or disgusted. Unlike the "newer" thinking and feeling brain segments, the primitive reptilian brain speaks the unfamiliar, but vastly important, language of *sensation*.

The language of sensations is, to many, a foreign language. There is a world of sensation and sensation-based feeling inside you that exists whether or not you are aware of it. Fortunately, it is a language that with a little practice is easy to learn. It's as essential to be familiar with sensations when traveling the "road to recovery from overwhelm and stress" as learning basic survival phrases when traveling abroad. In order to help your child, it only makes sense to get acquainted with your own inner landscape first. All it takes is some unhurried time, set aside without distractions, to pay attention to how your body feels. Sensations can range from pressure or temperature changes on the skin to vibrations, "butterflies," muscular tension, constriction or spaciousness, trembling or tingling and heat. This is the language of the lower brain that acts on our behalf when in danger or when unexpected change occurs. It has a very different focus than most of us are accustomed to. Its signals may seem imperceptible, subtle or strange at first because of our customary reliance on feedback from language, thought and emotion.

Because it is the reptilian brain that ensures our survival and homeostasis, it is the wise adult who befriends this deep instinctual layer of consciousness. No computers, equipment or costs are involved. All that is necessary is time, attention and intent. With some quiet, focused time this specialized language of sensation can easily be mastered. Below are several exercises to give you the "feel" for it. Remember: because the reptilian brain does not register words, you cannot learn its language merely by reading about it. Sensations *must* be experienced! Paradoxically, as we become more instinctual like the animals, we also become more fully human.

Getting Acquainted with Your Own Sensations

Although children may not be able to verbalize what they are feeling because they are too scared and/or too young to talk, they know *how* a shocking upset *feels* and so do you! It is the undeniable dread in the pit of the stomach, a racing heart, the tightness in the chest or the "lump in the throat." Turn on the news after a catastrophe or listen to a bystander who has just witnessed an accident describe his experience. "I don't have words for it." "It's such a cold feeling." "It was like getting the wind knocked out of me." "I just feel numb." "My heart wouldn't stop racing, but I couldn't move." "My legs were like lead."

Take a moment to think about your own experiences when something upsetting happened out of the blue. Can you recall some of the sensations you felt? Did your heart pound rapidly? Did you get dizzy? Did your throat or stomach tighten in a knot? And when the danger was over, how did the sensations gradually shift or change? Perhaps you noticed that you could breathe easier or felt some tingling or vibration as your muscles began to relax.

EXERCISE: NOTICING SENSATIONS

Let's try this brief experiment to get you started on deepening your awareness. Find a comfortable place to sit. Take some time to notice how you are feeling physically. Pay attention to your breathing. Are you comfortable or uncomfortable? *Where* in your body do you register your comfort level? What do you notice? Are you aware of your heart beating, or conscious of your breathing? Perhaps you're more aware of muscle tension or relaxation or the temperature of your skin; perhaps you notice sensations like "tingly." When you feel settled enough to go on, try the simple exercise below:

Imagine it's a pleasant summer day and you're driving with your kids to the beach. You are playing a favorite song and the family is singing along. You're not in a rush because it's your day off and you love being near the water. The kids will be taking a swimming lesson and you will be able to do whatever you want, free of responsibilities for an entire hour. Take a minute to notice how you are feeling right now—before you read the next paragraph. Note the sensations in various parts of your body, such as your belly, limbs, breath, muscles and skin. Also notice any thoughts or mental pictures you might have as you think about having free time at the beach.

*[**Note:** Pause here for a minute or two to give yourself enough time to notice your bodily sensations. When ready, continue with the second part of the story.]*

Suddenly, from out of nowhere, a hot-rod motorist cuts in front of you, nearly causing a collision. Furthermore, he is rude and shouts profanities at you, right in front of your kids, as if *you* had done something to cause the mishap. What are you noticing in your body and mind right now? Compare these feelings to the ones you had in the first part of the exercise. Pay attention to changes. What feels different now? Where does it feel different? Are you warm, hot or chilled? Do you feel tension or constriction anywhere? Notice changes in your heartbeat and breath. Notice if there is anything you feel like doing or saying. Or, do you just feel stunned?

There is no right or wrong way to answer. Each person has his or her own individual experience. You may have been scared and felt your shoulders, arms and hands tightening to turn the steering wheel quickly to swerve. Or, you might have blanked out and gone numb. When you imagined the other driver cursing at you, you might have felt irritated. If you did, where do you sense the irritation and what does it feel like? You may have noticed the muscles in your upper body tightening as your body prepared to fight. Or you might have noticed a word forming in your vocal cords to shout back, but the sounds never left your lips. When you check your body to feel your reactions and sensations in the present moment, you are experiencing your *basic instincts* of survival.

Now take a little time to let any activation (charged-up feelings) settle down. Think for a moment about the enclosed glass containers with a winter scene inside that you shake up to make white flakes that look like it's snowing. Remember that it takes a little time before all the flakes accumulate on the ground so that the "snowing" stops. In order for you to settle, it certainly doesn't help to get all shook up again. Instead, it takes a little quiet time of stillness and calm, just like with the snow scene, for the settling to occur. It can be very helpful to explore the room with your eyes, being aware that you are safe and that the visualization was only an exercise. As you continue to settle, place both feet flat on the floor to help you feel grounded. Next, direct your attention to something in the room that brings comfort, such as a flower, the color of the room, a tree or the sky outside the window, a photo or a favorite possession. Notice how you are feeling in your body at this moment *now*.

This brief exercise was intended to help you see that the language of sensation isn't really so foreign after all. Sitting around the dinner table, it's easy to feel a comfortable or overly stuffed stomach after a full meal or one that feels warm and cozy after sipping hot chocolate. But when people share their feelings, they typically express them as moods or emotions, such as happy, cranky, mad, excited or sad. Noticing sensations may seem odd at first, but the more you learn about the ups and downs of your own body's "moods," the more intuitive, instinctual and confident you will become. You may not know this, but your basic sense of well-being is based on your body's ability to regulate itself—rather than to escalate out of control. To be in control this way means to be open to that which occurs spontaneously within you. This capacity for self-regulation is enhanced by your ability to be aware of your changing sensations and to know what to do if unpleasant sensations remain stuck over time, thereby causing distress.

Building a New Vocabulary Together with Your Child

When learning skills with any new language, it helps to develop and practice the new vocabulary. Since the vocabulary of resilience is sensation, building a "sensation vocabulary" is a central skill crucial in developing resilience. The box below is provided to get you started. To create a balance, be sure to notice and label sensations that are pleasurable or neutral, as well as those that may be uncomfortable. You can have fun with your child adding to this list and watching it grow as you learn to both sense and name the strange new feelings from the world *inside* you!

SENSATION VOCABULARY BOX
- cold/warm/hot/chilly
- twitchy/butterflies
- sharp/dull/itchy
- shaky/trembly/tingly

- hard/soft/stuck
- jittery/icy/weak
- relaxed/calm/peaceful
- empty/full/dry/moist
- flowing/spreading
- strong/tight/tense
- dizzy/fuzzy/blurry
- numb/prickly/jumpy
- owie/tearful/goose-bumpy
- light/heavy/open
- tickly/cool/silky
- still/clammy/loose

Note that sensations are different than emotions. They describe the physical way the body feels. A non-verbal child who seems frightened can be invited to point to where in their body they might feel shaky or numb, or where the owie is.

"Pendulating" Between Pleasant and Unpleasant Sensations, Emotions and Images

In Somatic Experiencing® (the method developed by Dr. Peter Levine to prevent and heal trauma), the term "pendulation" refers to our natural rhythm of contraction and expansion. It is vital to know and *experience* this rhythm. Being familiar with it reminds us that no matter how bad we feel in the contraction phase, expansion *will inevitably* follow, bringing with it a sense of relief. One way to follow or "track" your body's own rhythm is as easy as paying attention to the pressure and flow of air in and out of your lungs and belly as you inhale and exhale. Notice if there is any tightness or whether the air seems to flow freely throughout your nostrils, throat, chest and belly. You might also note if the inhale and exhale are even or if one is shorter than the other. Are there pauses before the inhale and the exhale? How do the pauses feel? Do your muscles tense and relax as you breathe?

Rather than including only the expansion and contraction of the breath, however, pendulation is much more than that. It is the rhythm of our entire being as our internal state changes back and forth between uncomfortable sensations, emotions and images to more comfortable ones. This allows for new experiences to freshly emerge at each moment. When uncomfortable feelings don't readily go away, they are usually associated with stress or trauma. If we were defeated and frozen in hopelessness, the ability to move out of that state through natural pendulation will be diminished. We may need a little help to get the pendulum moving again. When this natural resilience process has been shut down, it must be gradually restored. The mechanisms that regulate our mood, vitality and health are dependent upon it. When this rhythm is re-established there is, at least, a tolerable balance between the pleasant and unpleasant. And no matter how bad a particular feeling may be, knowing that it can change releases you from a sentence of helplessness and hopelessness. And, as you assist your child with her natural rhythms, you are giving her a stable foundation for self-confidence.

EXERCISE: EXPLORING SENSATIONS AND THE RHYTHM OF PENDULATION

Note: You may wish to have a partner read the following story to you in a slow voice with plenty of pauses to give you a chance to develop more refined awareness. Another option is to record the story, listening to it privately or with someone else. In either case, it's best to approach this activity with an attitude of curiosity as you deepen your awareness of sensations and the pendulation of your own natural rhythm.

Take time to get comfortable in your chair. Notice where your body is touching the seat; notice how the chair supports your back and buttocks. Allow sufficient time to settle down into the chair. Notice your breathing and how you are feeling overall. As you slowly follow the story below, take the time to notice the sensations, thoughts, emotions and images that come up. Some will be subtle and others obvious. The more attention and time you take, the more your awareness will grow. At the same time it is important not to overdo it; it is recommended that you take no more than ten or fif-teen minutes with this exercise.

Now, imagine that today is your birthday. Even though it's a special day you feel lonely. You don't want to be alone so you decide to go see a movie. You start to get ready. As you reach for your wallet you have a dreadful feeling as you notice it is missing. What are you feeling? Take some time to notice feelings, sensations and thoughts in your body and your mind.

If you feel dread, what does it feel like? Where do you feel it in your body? Common places to experience sensations are: gut, chest, throat and the muscles in your neck and limbs. Do you feel a tightening or a sinking sensa-tion—perhaps queasiness? Do you notice any temperature changes in your hands? Do they feel sweaty, hot or cold? Is there any place you feel unsteady or wobbly? And notice how these sensations change over time as you attend to them. Does the intensity increase or decrease; does the tightening loosen or change to something else? Do the feelings spread or stay in one place?

As you settle, the thought comes to you that: "Oh, perhaps I left my wallet in the other room." Imagine that you go and look there. You check out other places you might have left it. You can't find it and you begin to get a bit fran-tic. Again, focus your attention inward and take time to notice your bodily sensations, your feelings and your thoughts.

Now, you slow down a bit and your thoughts become a little clearer. You begin to hunt for your wallet more methodically. Is it in the drawer? Maybe when I came in I left it over there on the table ... but then I went to the bath-room ... (you wonder) ... could I have left it in the bathroom; or was it at the supermarket? (Pause here to notice sensations.) However, while you're looking, you are interrupted by the ring of the telephone. You pick up the phone. It's your friend and she tells you that you left your wallet at her house. You take a big sigh of relief! Feel that and notice how you smile as you think about your previous frantic state of mind.

[Take plenty of time here, allowing your sensations to develop and be noticed before continuing with the story.]

Your friend tells you that she's leaving shortly, but she'll wait if you come right now. So you walk briskly to her house. Feel the strength in your legs as you walk fast. You arrive at her house and knock on her door, but there's no answer. You knock a second time and there's still no answer. You begin to think that you must have missed her. You feel a bit irritated. After all, she said that she would wait and you came as quickly as you could. Where do you feel the sensation of irritability? What does it feel like? Take your time and notice the range of sensations just as you did before. How do you experience the irritability? Where else do you feel it? What does it feel like?

From the back of the house, you hear your friend's muffled voice. She's telling you to come in. You open the door and it's really dark. You slowly find your way in the dark. You begin to make your way down the hallway. Notice how your body feels as you fumble through the darkness trying to get to the back of the house. You call again to your friend, but you're interrupted by a chorus of voices yelling, "Surprise!"

What are you feeling in your body now, *in this moment,* as you realize it's a surprise birthday party for you?! Again, take the time to notice your sensations, feelings and thoughts.

This exercise was intended to acquaint you with a variety of sensations, such as frustration, expectancy, relief, conflict and surprise. If you noticed different feeling states and were able to move smoothly from the pleasant to the unpleasant and back again, you now know what it feels like to pendulate.

The twists and turns of the visualization above were filled with many surprises. Surprise excites the nervous system. In the case of a good surprise, something gets registered in the body that makes you feel better. In the case of a horrifying surprise, distressing sensations may become stuck, resulting in a diminished sense of "OKness" and in feelings of helplessness. When you experience your sensations consciously, you can begin to move with fluidity out of one state and into another. Remember, whatever feels bad is never the final step. It is the movement from fixity to flow that frees us from the grip of trauma as we become more resilient and self-aware.

Ideally, you were able to feel this fluidity within yourself. If you did, you are well on your way to learning the skills that will help you to help your child fluidly glide through their sensations. If, in any way, you felt "stuck" or frozen on an unpleasant sensation, emotion, thought or disturbing image while practicing, take the time now to look around, get up, move and take notice of an object, movement, thought, person, pet or natural feature that makes you feel better. Take some time to sense how you know you are feeling better and where those sensations are located inside you. Then briefly "touch in" to the place in your body where you were previously stuck and notice what feelings you are having *now!*

EXERCISE: TRACKING SENSATIONS WITH A PARTNER

Often it is easier to concentrate on internal sensations when you have a partner to support you and help you focus just by being there. Choose someone you feel comfortable with and sit across from each other. The object of this exercise is to "track" sensations with a partner's quiet presence. Simply put, "tracking" means developing an awareness of your present state while noticing how sensations change moment by moment.

To begin, take time to reflect on something that happened today or yesterday that made you feel good about yourself or mildly upset. If you can't recall anything, you can simply notice how you are feeling as you get ready to try this exercise. As images, thoughts and emotions come and go, make note of them and what impact they have on your fluctuating sensations. Your partner's role is to track along with you. He may help you to become more aware of the details of your sensations. He can also keep you moving forward through time by an occasional gentle question—keeping pace with your rhythm—such as, "And when you feel..., what happens next?" After about ten to fifteen minutes of tracking, find a good place to stop and settle. Then switch places. Now you can practice helping your partner track sensations, creating safety with *your* quiet presence. You can also help him expand his awareness with a few well-placed questions, such as, "Where do you feel that? ... and what else do you notice?" Be sure to discuss what you discovered with each other afterwards.

Suggestion: Study the "Language of Sensation Idea Box" below with your partner before getting started. This box will help you remember to ask only those questions that "turn on" the instinctual part of the brain, rather than engaging the thinking brain that plans, analyzes and judges. Also, refrain from asking "Why?" questions for the same reason.

LANGUAGE OF SENSATION IDEA BOX

Your body-brain responds better to open-ended than closed-ended questions. An open-ended question invites curiosity. It suggests sensing rather than thinking. It defies a simple "yes" or "no" answer, which can be a communication dead-end. An example would be: "What do you notice in your body?" which summons a leisurely exploration and limitless answers. This is different than: "Are you feeling tense?" which forces a person to think rather than feel and then give a "yes" or "no" response.

Other examples of open-ended questions that you might consider when tracking sensations with your partner are listed below. These questions can be used judiciously from time to time to increase the ability to focus or to keep from getting stuck. For best results, use infrequently, allowing plenty of quiet time between each one. Allowing sufficient time is the key to developing sensory awareness. It's in the "quiet waiting" that our bodies begin to speak to us.

Open-Ended

- What do you notice in your body now?
- Where in your body do you feel that?
- What are you experiencing now?
- As you pay attention to that sensation, what happens next?
- How does it change?

Invitational

- What else are you noticing?
- Would you be willing to explore how your body might want to move?
- Would you be willing to focus on that feeling with a sense of curiosity about what might happen next?

Explore Sensation with Details to Increase Focus

- What are the qualities of that sensation?
- Does it have a size? Shape? Color? Weight?
- Does it spread? Notice the direction as it moves.
- Does the (pressure, pain, warmth, etc.) go from inward to outward or vice versa?
- Do you notice a center point? An edge? (Where does the sensation begin and end?)

Broaden Awareness of Sensation

- When you feel that, what happens in the rest of your body?
- When you feel that in your (part of the body), how does it affect you now?

Movement through Time

- What happens *next?* (Even if the person reports feeling "stuck")
- As you follow that sensation, where does it go? How does it change?
- Where does it move to (or want to move to if it could)?

Savoring and Deepening Sensations

- Allow yourself to enjoy that (warm, expansive, tingly, etc.) sensation as long as you'd like.

EXERCISE: MAKING A SENSATION TREASURE CHEST

Sensory awareness is a very important part of childhood development. It not only promotes intelligence and self-awareness, exploring the senses can provide family fun! The two easy activities described below will give your kids an opportunity to experiment with touch, taste and smell. You can make up your own explorations with sight and sound as well. So, shut off the TV and computer games and get started. All you'll need is pencil and paper to make notes after your experiments.

Activity 1

1. Find an empty box, can or bag in which to hide about a dozen objects.
2. Select items that have distinctly different textures such as: a feather, a piece of sandpaper, a variety of rocks of different shapes, sizes and textures, a cotton ball, a slimy toy, a piece of satin or silk fabric, steel wool, etc., and hide them in the box.
3. Have your child close his eyes (or use a blindfold) as he reaches in to pick an object, then tries to guess what it is by the way it feels. (This can also be a fun party game to be played at birthdays and other gatherings.)
4. Once all objects have been identified, have your child touch each object, then tell how it feels on his skin (tickly, prickly, cool, heavy, etc.).

5. Next, have your child compare the rocks of different weights by holding them in his hands and noticing how his muscles feel when a rock is *very* light, light, medium- heavy, heavy and *very* heavy.

6. Ask him to notice the difference he feels in his body when he touches something slimy as compared to something soft, etc. Have him point to the place in his body where he notices the difference. Is it in his arms, in his tummy, on his skin or in his throat?

7. Have your child ask you about differences that you might notice and take turns continuing to compare and contrast sensations.

8. Make a list of the sensations that he discovered.

Activity 2

1. Now try the above game using a "tasting tray" instead of a box. Fill tiny cups with a variety of edibles with different tastes and textures such as: sweet, salty, bitter, spicy, tart, crunchy, soft, etc.

2. Using a blindfold to avoid visual clues, have your child identify the various foods. You can give a cracker between each taste test to clear the palate.

3. As your child tastes each sample, have her tell you how the texture feels (creamy, hard, slippery, gooey, etc.) and then how the sample tastes and smells.

4. Now ask how each sample makes her tongue feel (tingly, prickly, cold, slippery, dry, relaxed, curled, numb, hot, etc.).

5. Repeat steps 6 and 7 from Activity 1, contrasting sensations caused by taste and smell rather than touch.

8. Make a list of the sensations that she discovered.

Activities like the ones above can help your family become acquainted with their sensations. It's a good idea to become familiar with your own sensations in a variety of situations, and to help your kids be aware of theirs, *before* an emergency occurs. Together you can increase your family's sensation vocabulary even more. It's easy to do. But like any new skill, training yourself to notice how you feel from moment to moment, especially after an upset has occurred, takes a bit of practice. And, with this practice of deepening your internal awareness, you will be ready to assist your child under almost any circumstance! In addition, you will also be better prepared for the unexpected shocks and strains as you navigate your own life. And remember, "it's never too late (for you) to have a happy childhood" . . . no matter how old you are.

It Doesn't Have to Hurt Forever

By now, if you have practiced the exercises, you realize that with time, intention, safety and awareness, unpleasant sensations *do* and *will* change. Overwhelm cannot always be prevented; bad things will happen. That is a fact of life. However, trauma can be prevented or transformed; it does not have to be a life sentence. The physiological "chain of events" within the body only becomes traumatic because of an incomplete process. Remember that this process is naturally inclined to complete itself whenever possible.

The sensation activities and ideas that you have now experienced were designed to help you to help your kids feel, tolerate and transform their sensations. Children become more resilient as their bodies learn how to return to balance in this way. When a child experiences something awful it can be devastating. However, when that same child experiences the triumph of moving out of the fear and frozenness back into life, a very special kind of self-confidence blossoms—the newfound feelings of resiliency and capability.

First Aid for Trauma Prevention: A Step-By-Step Guide

Assuming that you have practiced the exercises presented so far, you are now ready to learn how to guide your child after she has been exposed to a threatening, frightening or painful experience. Trauma prevention involves assisting your child to "unwind" the energy that was stirred up during her upset. There are eight steps involved in this procedure. They are simple to learn. They should be followed in the order that they are presented here. The first seven steps teach you how to help your child's body rebound from fear, shock and shut-down. Step 8 helps you to help your child recover emotionally, and to develop a coherent story of what happened. This final step helps your child put the bad occurrence in the past where it belongs. The eight simple steps outlined below can be used as soon as your child is in a safe, quiet place.

1. Check your own body's responses first.

Take time to notice your own level of fear or concern. Next, take a full deep breath, and as you exhale s-l-o-w-l-y feel the sensations in your own body. If you still feel upset, repeat until you feel settled. Feel your feet, ankles and legs, noticing how they make contact with the ground. Remember that any excess energy you have will help you to stay focused to meet the challenge at hand. The time it takes to establish a sense of calm is time well spent. It will increase your capacity to attend fully to your child. If you take the time to gather yourself, your own acceptance of whatever has happened will help you to attend to your child's needs. Your composure will greatly reduce the likelihood of frightening or confusing your child further. Remember, children are very sensitive to the emotional states of adults, particularly their parents.

2. Assess the situation.

If your child shows signs of shock (glazed eyes, pale skin, rapid or shallow pulse and breathing, disorientation, appears overly emotional or overly tranquil, i.e., acting like nothing has happened), do not allow him to jump up and return to play. You might say something like this: "Honey, you're safe now ... but you're still in shock (or a bit shaken up). Mommy/Daddy will stay right here with you until the shock wears off. It's important to stay still for a little while, even though you might want to play." Remember, a calm, confident voice communicates to your child that you know what's best.

3. As the shock wears off, guide your child's attention to his sensations.

Indications of coming out of shock that are easy to spot include some color returning to the skin, a slowing down and/or deepening of the breath, tears or some expression returning to the eyes (which may have seemed blank before). When you see one or more of these signs, softly ask your child how he feels "in his body." Next, repeat *his* or *her* answer as a question—"You feel okay in your body?"—and wait for a nod or other response. Be more specific with the next question: "How do you feel in your tummy (head, arm, leg, etc.)?" If he mentions a distinct sensation (such as "It feels tight or hurts"), gently ask about its location, size, shape, color or weight (e.g. heavy or light). Keep guiding your child to stay with the present moment with questions such as, "How does the rock (sharpness, lump, 'owie,' sting) feel now?" If he is too young or too startled to talk, have him point to where it hurts. (Remember that children tend to describe sensations with metaphors such as "hard as a rock" or "butterflies.")

4. Slow down and follow your child's pace by careful observation of changes.

Timing is everything! This may be the hardest part for the adult; but it's the most important part for the child. Providing a minute or two of silence between questions allows deeply restorative physiological cycles to engage. Too many questions asked too quickly disrupt the natural course that leads to resolution. Your calm presence and patience are sufficient to facilitate the movement and release of excess energy.

This process cannot be rushed. Be alert for cues that let you know a cycle has finished. If uncertain whether a cycle has been completed, wait and watch for your child to give you clues. Examples of signs include a deep, relaxed, spontaneous breath, the cessation of crying or trembling, a stretch, a yawn, a smile or the making of eye contact.

The completion of this cycle may not mean that the recovery process is over. Wait to see if another cycle begins or if there is a sense of enough for now. Keep your child focused on sensations for a few more minutes just to make sure the process is complete.

If your child seems tired, stop. There will be other opportunities later to complete the process.

5. Keep validating your child's physical responses.

Resist the impulse to stop your child's tears or trembling, while reminding him that whatever has happened is over and that he will be OK. Your child's reactions need to continue until they stop on their own. This part of the natural cycle usually takes from one to several minutes. Studies have shown that children who are able to cry and tremble after an accident have fewer problems recovering from it over the long term.[2] Your task is to convey to your child through word and touch that crying and trembling are normal, healthy reactions! A reassuring hand on the back, shoulder or arm, along with a few gently spoken words as simple as "That's OK" or "That's right, just let the scary stuff shake right out of you" will help immensely.

6. Trust in your child's innate ability to heal.

As you become increasingly comfortable with your own sensations, it will be easier to relax and follow your child's lead. Your primary function, once the process has begun, is to not disrupt it! Trust your child's innate ability to heal. Trust your own ability to allow this to happen. If it helps you in letting go, take a moment to reflect on and feel the presence of a higher power or the remarkable perfection of nature guiding you in the ordinary miracle of healing. Your job is to "stay with" your child. Your balanced presence makes a safe container for your child to release her tears, fears and any strange new feelings. Use a calm voice and reassuring hand to let your child know that she is on the right track. To avoid unintentional disruption of the process, don't shift the child's position, distract her attention, hold her too tightly or position yourself too close or too far away for comfort. Notice when your child begins to look around to see what's happening with a sense of curiosity. This type of checking out the surroundings is called "orienting" and is a sign of resolution. It is a sign of completion, or letting go, of the stressful energy produced in response to the scary event. A natural orientation to what's happening in the environment may bring with it more sensory awareness, aliveness in the present moment and even feelings of joy.

7. Encourage your child to rest even if she doesn't want to.

Deep discharge and processing of the event generally continue during rest and sleep. Do not stir up discussion about the mishap by asking questions about it during this stage. Later on, though, your child may want to tell a story about what happened, draw a picture or play it through. If a lot of energy was mobilized, the release will continue. The next cycle may be too subtle for you to notice, but this resting stage promotes a fuller recovery, allowing the body to gently vibrate, give off heat and go through skin color changes, etc., as the nervous system returns to relaxation and equilibrium. In addition, dream activity can help move the body through the necessary physiological changes. These changes happen naturally. All you have to do is provide a calm, quiet environment. (**Caution:** Of course, if your child possibly has had a head injury, you want her to rest but *not* sleep until your doctor tells you that it's safe.)

8. The final step is to attend to your child's emotional responses and help him or her make sense of what happened.

Later, when your child is rested and calm—even the next day—set aside some time for him to talk about his feelings and what he experienced. Begin by asking him to tell you what happened. Children often feel anger, fear, sadness, worry, embarrassment, shame or guilt. Help your child to know that those feelings are OK and that you understand. Tell the child about a time when you or someone you know had a similar experience and/or felt the same way. This will encourage expression of what your child is feeling. It also helps him not to feel weird or defective in some way because of what happened or because of his reactions. Let your child know by your actions that *whatever* he is feeling is accepted by you and worthy of your time and attention. Set aside some time for story-telling or for relating the details of the incident to assess if there are any residual feelings. Drawing, painting and working with clay can be very helpful in releasing strong emotions. If you notice your child becoming unduly upset at any point, again have him attend to his sensations in order to help the distress pass. You can assist your child to continue the recovery process through play at this stage. Play, as you will learn with the story of Sammy in the next chapter, works especially well with children who do not yet talk or are too shook-up to speak. Additionally, you will learn how art activities and silly rhythms that you and your child can make up can be a fun way to promote further healing at the emotional level.

Now that you know what needs to be done, the next step is to in-crease your skill in doing it. The information that follows shows you how to select your words, pace and tone of voice to de-activate the "trauma charge." Once you gain the ability to do this, you have the power to instill confidence that all is well, rather than unwittingly causing unnecessary fright.

Attuning to Your Child's Rhythms, Sensations and Emotions

How can adults give appropriate support to set the healing process in motion? After assuring your child that any powerful emotions that she may be having are normal, it's important to help your child understand that the distress she is feeling will go away.

Children are comforted and empowered by knowing that it won't hurt forever and that you will stay with them until they begin to feel more like themselves again. Actually, kids tend to move through their feelings rather quickly when they are not hurried or inhibited by an adult's time schedule. Being "attuned" means hav-ing the patience to withstand your child's uncomfortable emotions rather than distracting him from them or suggesting that he should just get over it. It also means pacing yourself at the speed that suits your child. This gives him the permission to be genuine.

The importance of this acceptance and respect is not to be underestimated. Just like the splint sets a broken arm properly, your undivided attention and soothing, non-judgmental language set the conditions for your child, in his or her own time, to rebound to a healthy sense of well-being. And just as the mending of the bone happens on its own timetable, so does the mending of your child's psyche.

We want to emphasize again that children read their parents' facial, postural and vocal cues, so it is very important that you are aware of what your body language is saying. Often children react the way they think their parents expect them to because of a desire to please, to avoid criticism and scolding, or to do the "right" thing. They may act "strong" and "brave," overriding their own feelings only to end up with trauma symptoms that could have been avoided. Countless adults in therapy have reported stifling their feelings as children to protect their parents from feeling bad. Sometimes their "brave face" is an attempt to reduce the anxiety of a bewildered parent.

How to Avoid the Pitfall of Overriding Your Child's Needs

The *first step* is to be alert to the possibility of your own feelings of terror or vulnerability when something unexpected happens. The *second step* is to connect with your own body. When you are momentarily "beside yourself" you literally need to get back inside yourself. Ideally, you will be prepared by what you learned from the previous exercises. Perform emotional first aid on yourself; take the time to notice how your feet contact the floor. Are the soles of your feet feeling supported solidly by the ground? Can you feel the weight and strength of your lower legs or do you hardly feel them? Do you feel planted and stable or like you could be knocked off center easily? How do your arms and hands feel? The more experienced you are at being aware of your own sensations, the easier and quicker this brief check-in period will be.

If you need more stability, bend your knees to lower your center of gravity and sway back and forth or dance slowly, moving your ankle joints and pelvis until you feel more energy in the lower half of your body. As you become more grounded and check your new sensations, you may be pleasantly surprised to experience a spontaneous breath and a feeling of being back on center. It is amazing how these two simple steps can make it easier to be fully present with your child. It's the same idea as with the announcement made by the flight attendant to bring the oxygen mask to your nose and mouth first and then assist your child with her mask.

By tending to yourself first, paradoxically, you are in a better position to tend to your child. When you can feel your center, can notice that your breath slows down and you experience the fluidity of changing sensations, you have moved out of a momentary "freeze." Your energy is now available to pay close attention to your child's needs and expression. In this way you will naturally circumvent complicating your child's reactions with your own.

Of course, it is easier to be calm when you've had some practice recovering from your own stressful or frightening situations using what you have learned so far to complete and discharge the energy from any incomplete responses. You can begin by applying your internal awareness with small incidents that happen during the course of an ordinary day. Sometimes it can be helpful to observe how others calmly handle emergency situations, especially if you grew up in a chaotic family and have never observed a model of composure. When a parent's body language and words convey safety, it's amazing how quickly kids can return from an altered state of shock and shake off the excess "emergency" energy. The following example of "emotional first aid" clearly illustrates how a calm adult presence can facilitate completion of a discharge cycle after a terrifying accident.

A teenager on a motorcycle had been struck by a car and knocked off his bike on the city street. He hit his head, but luckily he was wearing a helmet. His arms and legs were scraped badly. Most obvious was his pale skin, wide eyes and altered state. The teen crawled, in shock, to the curb. After a passerby was asked to call an ambulance, I took a moment to feel my breath and heart settle from what I had just witnessed. As I noticed that the teen was alive and able to move, I placed my attention on my breath, lower legs and feet settling a little more. I kept in mind that the most important trait I needed to assist this injured stranger in coming out of shock was my own calm presence. I sat down on the curb next to the young man and simply said, "There's an ambulance on its way" in a very calm voice. Knowing the importance of emotional first aid and what needs to be done to help, I said (with a soft voice of authority and confidence), "You're in shock. I'll stay right here with you until the ambulance comes; you're alive and you're going to be okay." As soon as I finished my sentence, the teen began shaking. I placed my hand firmly but gently on the muscles of his upper arm (deltoid) and encouraged his spontaneous sensations: "That's right ... just let it all go ... let the shaking happen ... you're doing good ... you're going to be fine." Three minutes later the color returned to the teenager's face. Soon his shaking changed to gentle trembling and he released a few tears. A spontaneous breath came all of a sudden and he looked around to survey what had just happened. He was returning to his senses, to himself!

The critical idea here is that when we are vulnerable, we benefit most from feeling a connection with a calm person who is confident of what to do and is able to convey a sense of safety and compassion. Your child will feel safe if he knows that you are strong enough to withstand (contain) his shock without becoming over-whelmed yourself.

Remember that "shock energy" is survival energy and can be frightening as it is being released. The parent becomes the "container" of this energy by keeping present and grounded in the knowledge that this is a normal process and their child will be alright.

Another thing to know when assisting your child following an emergency is the importance of rhythm and timing. Think about it—everything in the wild is dictated by cycles. The seasons turn, the moon waxes and wanes, tides ebb and flow, the sun rises and sets. Animals follow the rhythms of nature in their mating, birthing and hibernating rituals. This is in direct relationship to nature's pendulum. We also resolve overwhelm through the natural cycles of *expansion and contraction.* This tells us that no matter how badly we are feeling right now, this contraction *will* be followed by an expansion toward freedom.

But for human beings, these rhythms pose a two-fold challenge. First, compared to our video game and BlackBerry world, they move at a much slower pace than we are accustomed to. Second, they are entirely beyond our control. Healing cycles require an open receptivity as they are observed and respected; they cannot be evaluated, manipulated, hurried or changed. When given the time and attention needed, children are able to complete their own healing cycles.

Resolving a stress reaction does much more than eliminate the likelihood of developing trauma later in life. It also fosters an abil-ity to move through any threatening situation with greater ease and flexibility. It creates, in essence, a natural resilience to stress. A nervous system accustomed to experiencing and releasing stress is healthier than a nervous system burdened with an ongoing, if not accumulating, level of stress. Children who are encouraged to attend to their instinctual responses are rewarded with a lifelong legacy of health and vigor!

CHAPTER III

———

Tricks of the Trade:
Restoring Resilience through
Play, Art and Rhymes

*"You can discover more about a person
in an hour of play than in a year of conversation."*
– Plato

Often with minor accidents, falls and other "ordinary events," applying the basic first aid skills you learned in Chapter II is sufficient to help your child rebound. Sometimes, however, traumatic effects may be minimized but not entirely prevented. This is especially true with more frightening situations like invasive medical procedures, prolonged or permanent separation from parents, accidents that involve extreme terror and horror, witnessing violence or being the victim of abuse. In these cases, professional mental health services can be invaluable and, at times, necessary. Even so, there is much that parents can do to help reduce their child's stress and anxiety. By using the guided play, art activities and rhymes you will learn in this chapter, you can bolster your child's confidence in coping with the lumps and bumps of life.

Without words, young children sometimes show parents the parts of their experience that have overwhelmed them. Toddlers, preschoolers and elementary school children easily express their worst fears and unconscious turmoil through their world of make-believe, play and art. If your child plays aggressively with toys, setting up the same scene over and over, such as one doll hurting another doll, she may be trying to recover from a frightening situation. Or she may have witnessed something scary happening to someone else. In this case, help from a parent to move the play from repetition to resolution can relieve her distress.

On the other hand, sometimes children don't show us their hurts in such obvious ways. They may avoid any activity, person or other reminder that resembles what originally frightened them. Sometimes the child's new behavior, although anything but subtle, is a mystery. The bewildered family might not connect his conduct with the source of his terror. This was the case with Sammy, whom you will read about shortly.

Rather than expressing themselves in easy-to-understand ways, kids frequently show us that they are suffering in terribly frustrating ways. They may act "bratty," clinging to parents or throwing tantrums. Or they might struggle with agitation, hyperactivity, nightmares or sleeplessness. Such symptoms can try one's patience, especially when caregivers don't have a clue what is causing their child to behave in such unpredictable and disturbing ways.

More troubling, kids may act out their worries and hurts by wielding a false sense of power, steam-rolling over a younger, weaker child or pet. Sometimes children do not find an outlet of expression. Their distress may show up as head and tummy aches or bed-wetting. Another signal may be shunning people and things they used to enjoy. Or your child may try to control his environment and the people around him in order to manage unbearable anxiety.

What can parents do to help relieve and resolve the feelings of fear, betrayal and shame that may underlie their child's puzzling behavior? Since children by their nature enjoy play, you can help them to rebound through "guided play." The steps you will learn in this section will help your child move beyond his fears and gain mastery over his scariest moments. Whether your child's behavior is a mystery or she is engaging in play reminiscent of her trauma, the following account will help you to help her.

As you take a look at the following story of Sammy, a little boy who is not yet three years old, you will see how setting up a "play session" can lead to a reparative experience with a victorious outcome. With the guidance provided after the story, you will be able to give similar support to your child. The following is an example of what can happen when an ordinary fall, requiring a visit to the emergency room for stitches, goes awry. It also shows how several months later, Sammy's terrifying experience was transformed through play into a renewed sense of confidence and joy.

THE STORY OF SAMMY

Sammy has been spending the weekend with his grandparents, where I am their guest. He is being an impossible tyrant, aggressively and relentlessly trying to control his new environment. Nothing pleases him; he displays a foul temper every waking moment. When he is asleep, he tosses and turns as if wrestling with his bedclothes. This behavior is not entirely unexpected from a two-and-a-half-year-old whose parents have gone away for the weekend—children with separation anxiety often act it out. Sammy, however, has always enjoyed visiting his grandparents, and this behavior seems extreme to them.

They confide to me that six months earlier, Sammy fell off his high chair and split his chin open. Bleeding heavily, he was taken to the local emergency room. When the nurse came to take his temperature and blood pressure, he was so frightened that she was unable to record his vital signs. The child was then strapped down in a "pediatric papoose" (a board with flaps and Velcro straps). With his torso and legs immobilized, the only parts of his body he could move were his head and neck—which, naturally, he did, as energetically as he could. The doctors responded by tightening the restraint and immobilizing his head with their hands in order to suture his chin.

After this upsetting experience, mom and dad took Sammy out for a hamburger and then to the playground. His mother was very attentive and showed her son that she truly understood how scary and painful the ordeal was for him. Soon, all seemed forgotten. However, the boy's overbearing attitude began shortly afterwards. Could Sammy's tantrums and controlling behavior be related to his perceived helplessness from this trauma? I discovered that Sammy had been to the emergency room several times with various injuries, though he had never displayed this degree of terror and panic. When his parents returned, we agreed to explore whether there might be a traumatic charge still associated with this recent episode.

We all gathered in the cabin where I was staying. With parents, grandparents and Sammy watching, I placed his stuffed Pooh Bear on the edge of a chair in such a way that it immediately fell to the floor. We decided that it was hurt and had to be taken to the hospital. Sammy shrieked, bolted for the door and ran across a footbridge and down a narrow path to the creek. Our suspicions were confirmed. His most recent visit to the hospital was neither harmless nor forgotten. Sammy's behavior told us that this game was potentially overwhelming for him.

Sammy's parents brought him back from the creek. He clung frantically to his mother as we prepared for another game. We reassured him that we would all be there to help protect Pooh Bear. Again he ran—but this time only into the next room. We followed him in there and waited to see what would happen next. Sammy ran to the bed and hit it with both arms while looking at me expectantly.

"Mad, huh?" I said. He gave me a look that confirmed my question. Interpreting his expression as a go-ahead sign, I put Pooh Bear under a blanket and placed Sammy on the bed next to him. "Sammy, let's all help Pooh Bear." I held Pooh Bear under the blanket and asked everyone to help. Sammy watched with interest but soon got up and ran to his mother. With his arms held tightly around her legs, he said, "Mommy, I'm scared."

Without pressuring Sammy, we waited until he was ready and willing to play the game again. The next time Grandma and Pooh

Bear were held down together, and Sammy actively participated in their rescue. When Pooh Bear was freed, Sammy ran to his mother, clinging even more tightly than before. He began to tremble and shake in fear, and then, dramatically, his chest opened up in a growing sense of excitement and pride. *Here we see the transition between traumatic re-enactment and healing play.* The next time he held on to mommy, there was less clinging and more excited jumping.

We waited until Sammy was ready to play again. Everyone except Sammy took a turn being rescued with Pooh. Each time, Sammy became more vigorous as he pulled off the blanket and escaped into the safety of his mother's arms. When it was Sammy's turn to be held under the blanket with Pooh Bear, he became quite agitated and fearful. He ran back to his mother's arms several times before he was able to accept the ultimate challenge. Bravely, he climbed under the blankets with Pooh while I held the blanket gently down. I watched his eyes grow wide with fear, *but only for a moment this time.* Then he grabbed Pooh Bear, shoved the blanket away and flung himself into his mother's arms. Sobbing and trembling, he screamed, "Mommy, get me out of here! Mommy, get this thing off of me!" His startled father told me that these were the *exact words* Sammy screamed while imprisoned in the papoose at the hospital. He remembered this clearly because he had been quite surprised by his son's ability to make such a direct, well-spoken demand at such a young and tender age.

We went through the escape several more times. Each time Sammy exhibited more power and more triumph. Instead of running fearfully to his mother, he jumped excitedly up and down. With every successful escape, we all clapped and danced together, cheering, "Yeah for Sammy, yeah yeah! Sammy saved Pooh Bear!" Two-and-a-half-year-old Sammy had achieved mastery over the experience that had shattered him a few months earlier. The trauma-driven, aggressive, foul-tempered behavior used in an attempt to control his environment disappeared. And his "hyperactive" and avoidant behavior during the reworking of his medical trauma was transformed into triumphant play.

Four Principles to Guide Children's Play Toward Resolution

The following analysis of Sammy's play experience is designed to help you understand and apply the following principles when working with your own children.

1. Let the child control the pace of the game.

In the last chapter, you learned the importance of attuning to your child's needs. Healing takes place in a moment-by-moment slowing down of time. That is true for everyone! Your child's pace may be very different from yours. In order to help your child feel safe, follow her pace and rhythm; don't subject her to yours. If you put yourself in your child's "shoes" through careful observation of her behavior, you will learn quickly how to resonate with her. Let's look at Sammy's behavior.

What Sammy "Told" Us

By running out of the room when Pooh Bear fell off the chair, Sammy told us quite clearly that he was not ready to engage in this new activating "game."

What We Did to Help Sammy Feel Safe

Sammy had to be "rescued" by his parents, comforted and brought back to the scene before continuing. We all had to assure Sammy that we would be there to help protect Pooh Bear. By offering this support and reassurance, we helped Sammy move closer to playing the game.

What Sammy "Told" Us

When Sammy ran into the bedroom instead of out the door, he was telling us that he felt less threatened and more confident of our support. Children may not state verbally whether they want to continue, so take cues from their behavior and responses. Respect their wishes in whatever way they choose to communicate. Children should never be forced to do more than they are willing and able to do.

What You Can Do to Help Your Child

Slow down the process if you notice signs of fear, constricted breathing, stiffening or a dazed (dissociated) demeanor. These reactions will dissipate if you simply wait quietly and patiently while reassuring your child that you are still by their side and on their side. Usually, your youngster's eyes and breathing will tell you when it's time to continue.

EXERCISE

Read Sammy's story again and pay particular attention to the places that indicate his decision to continue the game. There are three explicit examples in addition to the one cited above.

---

2. Distinguish among fear, terror and excitement.

Experiencing fear or terror for more than a brief moment during guided play usually will not help the child move through the trauma. Most children will take action to avoid such overwhelming feelings. Let them! At the same time you are helping to bring the child back to, and "touch-into," the challenging sensations and feelings they are trying to avoid, but without being overwhelmed. Try to discern whether he is avoiding or has accessed his fear and made an empowered escape. The following is a clear-cut example to help you develop the skill of "reading" when a break is needed and when it's time to guide the momentum forward.

What Sammy "Told" Us

When Sammy ran down to the creek, he was demonstrating avoidance behavior. In order to resolve his traumatic reaction, Sammy had to feel that he was in control of his actions rather than driven to act by his emotions.

How to "Read" Your Child's Experience

Avoidance behavior occurs when fear and terror threaten to overwhelm your child. This behavior is usually accompanied by some sign of emotional distress (crying, frightened eyes, screaming). Active escape, on the other hand, is potentially exhilarating. Children become excited by their small triumphs and often show pleasure by glowing with smiles, clapping their hands or laughing heartily. Overall, the response is much different from avoidance behavior. Excitement is evidence of the child's successful discharge of the emotions that accompanied the original bad experience. This is positive, desirable and necessary.

Trauma is transformed by changing intolerable feelings and sensations into bearable or even pleasurable ones. For instance, it is not unusual for high anxiety to turn into exuberance because both have a similar level of activation in the nervous system.

How to Support Your Child

If your child appears excited, it is OK to offer encouragement and to continue as we did when we clapped and danced with Sammy. However, if your child appears frightened or cowed, give reassurance but don't encourage any further movement at that time. Be present with your full attention and support; wait patiently while the fear subsides. If your child shows signs of fatigue, take a rest break.

3. Take one small step at a time.

You can never move too slowly in renegotiating a traumatic event. Traumatic play is repetitious almost by definition. Make use of this cyclical characteristic. The key difference between *"renegotiation"* and traumatic play is that in renegotiation there are incremental differences in the child's responses and behaviors in moving toward mastery and resolution.

What Sammy "Told" Us
When Sammy ran into the bedroom instead of out the door, he was responding with a different behavior indicative that progress had been made.

Monitoring Your Child's Progress
No matter how many repetitions it takes, if your child is responding differently—such as with a slight increase in excitement, with more speech or with more spontaneous movements—he is moving through the trauma. If the child's responses appear to be moving in the direction of compulsive repetition instead of expansion and variety, you may be attempting to move too fast, causing too much arousal for your child to make progress.

How to Help Your Child Take One Small Step at a Time
Ground yourself and pay attention to your sensations until your own breathing brings a sense of calm, confidence and spontaneity. Slow down the rate of change by breaking the play into smaller increments. This may seem contradictory to what was stated earlier about following your child's pace. However, it is the wise parent who will prevent her child from getting too agitated and overwhelmed. In order to do this, you may need to slow down the pace of the game.

If your child appears wound up, it's OK to invite some healing steps. For example, after a medical trauma you might say, "Let's see, I wonder what we can do so (Pooh Bear, Dolly, etc.) doesn't get scared before you (the pretend doctor/nurse) give him a shot?" Often children will come up with creative solutions that demonstrate exactly what kind of care or reassurance was missing from *their* experience.

Don't be concerned about how many times you have to go through what seems to be the same old thing. (We engaged Sammy in playing the game with Pooh Bear at least ten times. Sammy was able to renegotiate his traumatic responses fairly quickly. Your child might require more time.) You don't need to do it all in one day! Resting and time help your child to internally reorganize his experience at subtle levels. If the resolution is not complete, your child will return to a similar phase when given the opportunity to continue the play at another time.

If these suggestions don't seem to help, re-read this chapter and look closely at the possible role you are playing and observe more carefully how your child is responding. Perhaps you are becoming frustrated, unduly frightened or possibly missing some of your child's signals. It takes practice to be in sync with subtleties. Once your child begins responding, forget your concerns and enjoy the game!

4. Become a safe container

Remember that nature is on your side. For the parent, perhaps the most difficult and important aspect of assisting your child in transforming a traumatic event is maintaining your own belief that things *will* turn out OK. This feeling comes from inside you and is projected out to your child. It becomes a container that surrounds the child with a feeling of confidence. This may be particularly difficult if your child resists your attempts to help him.

If your child resists, be patient and reassuring. The instinctive part of your child wants to rework her experience. All you have to do is wait for that part to feel confident and safe enough to assert itself. If you are excessively worried about your own capability to help your child, you may inadvertently send a message to your child that she needs to help *you* curb *your* anxiety. Adults with their own unresolved trauma may be particularly susceptible to falling into this trap. If the process continues to be frustrating don't push it. Instead, find a professional play therapist to help your child; and please don't procrastinate in seeking help for yourself!

Discussion: What Might Happen to Children Who Don't Receive Help?

If Sammy hadn't received help, would he have become more anxious, hyperactive, clinging and controlling? Or would his trauma possibly have resulted in bed-wetting or in avoidant behaviors later? Would he have developed physical symptoms like tummy aches, migraine headaches and anxiety attacks without knowing why? All of these speculations are possible, and equally impossible to pin down. We cannot know how, when or even whether a child's traumatic experience will invade his or her life in another form. However, we can help protect our children from these possibilities through prevention. This "ounce of prevention" will, in any case, help them develop into more confident and spontaneous adults.

Children like Sammy rarely get help directly following an incident such as this one. *You* are the pioneer parents in this regard. You will learn that youngsters can easily be supported at this critical time while they literally tremble and "shake out" the immobility, shame, loss and rage from their terrifying experiences. Through guided play, children can safely discharge the intense energy mobilized in a failed attempt to defend against a frightening and painful experience. But they must do this with your support, guidance and protection.

Discussion: What's the Difference between Traumatic Play and Therapeutic Play?

It is important to appreciate the differences among avoidance of reminders of the event, play that repetitiously mimics the trauma and the actual re-working of the trauma, like what we saw with Sammy. Traumatized adults often re-enact an event that in some way represents, at least to their unconscious, the original trauma. For example, a victim of childhood sexual abuse might become promiscuous or be a sex offender or perhaps avoid the possibility of sex altogether.

Similarly, children re-create parts of the event that frightened them. While they may not be aware of the significance behind their behaviors, they are deeply driven by the feelings associated with the original trauma. Even if they won't talk about the trauma, traumatic play is one way a child will tell his or her story. It is a sure clue that your child is still disturbed.

The example that follows best portrays this type of "troubled" play. In *Too Scared to Cry,* Lenore Terr describes the responses of three-and-a-half-year-old Lauren as she plays with toy cars. "The cars are going on the people," Lauren says as she zooms two racing cars toward some finger puppets. "They're pointing their pointy parts into the people. The people are scared. A pointy part will come on their tummies, and in their mouths, and on their . . . [she points to her skirt]. My tummy hurts. I don't want to play anymore."[1]

Lauren stops herself as her bodily sensation of fear abruptly surfaces. This is a typical reaction. She may return over and over to the same play, each time stopping when the fearful sensations in her tummy become uncomfortable. Some therapists would argue that Lauren is using her play as an attempt to gain some control over the situation that traumatized her. Her play does resemble "exposure" treatments used routinely to help adults overcome phobias. But Terr cautions that such play ordinarily doesn't yield much success. Even if it does serve to reduce a child's distress, this process is quite slow in producing results. Most often, the play is compulsively repeated without resolution. Unresolved, repetitious, traumatic play can reinforce the traumatic impact in the same way that re-enactment and cathartic reliving of traumatic experiences can reinforce trauma in adults.

The re-working or renegotiation of a traumatic experience, as we saw with Sammy, represents a process that is fundamentally different from traumatic play or re-enactment. Left to their own devices, most children will attempt to avoid the traumatic feelings that their play evokes. With guidance, *Sammy was able to "live his feelings through" by gradually and sequentially mastering his fear.* Using this stepwise re-working of the traumatic event together with Pooh Bear's companionship, Sammy was able to emerge as the victor and hero. A sense of triumph and heroism almost always signals the successful conclusion of a renegotiated traumatic event. By slowly and deliberately following Sammy's lead after setting up a disturbing scene, joining in his play and making the game up as we went along, Sammy got to let go of his fear. It took very little adult direction (about half an hour) and support to achieve the unspoken goal of helping him to successfully "escape," thereby experiencing a very different outcome than was possible in the emergency room.

Does Your Child Need Extra Help?

To find out if your child's troubling behavior is unresolved, try mentioning the frightening episode and observe her responses. A traumatized child may not want to be reminded of the predisposing event. Once reminded, she may become agitated or fearful. Sometimes your child may leave the room because she doesn't want to talk about it; while another child may be unable to stop talking about it. And children who have "outgrown" unusual behavior patterns have not necessarily discharged the energy that gave rise to them. The reason traumatic reactions can hide for years is that the maturing nervous system is able to control the excess energy by sheer will, at least temporarily. By reminding your child of a frightening incident that precipitated altered behaviors in years past, you may well stir up signs of traumatic residue.

You may be wondering, "Why stir up the past—especially if my child's behavior is under control?" Reactivating a traumatic symptom need not necessarily be cause for concern. Rather, it is an opportunity to discharge any residual traumatic energy and complete the process. This helps to greatly reduce accumulated stress while restoring optimal functioning of reflexes, balance, coordination, grounding, assertiveness and sense of self. It is a direct path to instilling resilience and increasing confidence and joy.

As you assist your child through stressful times and overwhelming situations, we want to caution you that sometimes professional help is needed. Although often parents can help their child recover their confidence after an accident, fall or simple medical procedure, even the most skilled parents cannot resolve everything. This is especially true with more complex situations, such as molestation (especially by a family member). No matter what the event, if your child is having a reaction that lingers after you have given it your best shot, again, it is advantageous to seek help.

On the other hand, if your child's issue is not resolved in one sitting, that doesn't necessarily mean that you need a professional. Some children require a few more "play" sessions with you to really turn things around. If, however, after repeated attempts your child remains insecure or frozen and does not move toward triumph and mastery, **DO NOT** force the issue. Consult qualified help from a professional experienced in working with children. While preventing trauma in children may be somewhat easy, healing trauma in children can, at times, be complex. This is especially true when there were multiple events, the stressor was prolonged and/or the youngster was unsupported at that time. As mentioned, trauma becomes increasingly complicated if the child was betrayed by a trusted adult.

More Help for Kids through "Make-Believe" Play

In addition to making up scenes with stuffed animals and dolls, like "Pooh" and teddy bears, lots of different types of toys can be enlisted. Kids love puppets and making up stories that their puppets can act out on a makeshift stage. This is especially true for children too frightened to work directly on whatever it was that happened to them. For kids over three (because of choking haz-ard if younger), small toy figures are an ideal way to engage in set-ting up play scenes. Dramatic play that includes "dress-up" and role-play also can be a window into helping your child sort through difficult emotions and sensations.

Puppets

The cool thing about puppets is that they have strong appeal to kids of all ages, even teens. It is not unusual for adolescents to pick them up just "to mess around" and then eventually start playing with them. It is fun to get very silly together with your child. It's easy to begin by talking in different voices and tones without any specific goal. Encourage spontaneity by being spontaneous your-self. This puppet play gives kids enough psychological distance from their problems, creating safety to express themselves freely. Children who have difficulty feeling and sharing their emotions can almost always have an indirect outlet through the puppets.

After a time of unguided play, you can lead your child in a direc-tion that helps him deal either with the situation that originally caused the distress or with the behavior that follows. If your child, for example, developed symptoms such as bottling up her anger by becoming sulky or depressed, you can guide her to express those feelings through the puppets. You do this by modeling anger through the puppet yourself. For example, "Alice the Angry Alli-gator" can gnash her teeth and loudly exclaim whatever is bugging her. On the other hand, if your child acts out his anger by bopping other kids on the head or having tantrums, "Angus the Angry Giant" can stomp his feet and announce to the whole kingdom what it feels like to be mad. In this way your child can express himself without hurting anyone. Kids can communicate their fears, sadness and joy as well. During this kind of play, not only are emo-tions conveyed, but often children come up with the dandiest cre-ative solutions to their problems.

As parents become more relaxed with this type of connection through play, you can take a step closer to the actual situation (if it is known). For example, Mom or Dad can have one of the puppets fall, be in a car crash, talk about an upcoming surgical procedure, be approached in a way that is frightening or mention what it felt like when Grandpa died. Sensations, thoughts and emotions can be explored through the puppets. Children are amazingly resilient when adults set up the right circumstances. They will begin to face their fears and gain mastery over the situations that have disempowered them.

Puppets can be made or purchased. Some fit on the whole hand; others on one finger. You can buy them at toy stores and in the toy sections of department stores such as Target. They can also be purchased online from www.puppetuniverse.com and www.the PuppetStore.com. Or it can be fun to make them with your child. Brown paper bags or old socks can be used as an inexpensive alternative to buying puppets. Simply have your child use colored markers to make the face. Eyes and mouth can be cut out with scissors. Ears and hair can be made from paper scraps or yarn and pasted on with a glue stick if desired. For finger puppets, an empty shoe box can serve as a stage. For larger puppets, a large box or small table will suffice.

Miniature Toys

Playing with small toys or figurines (for children over three years of age) is another rich entrance into the inner world of an upset child. With the growing number of computer and video games together with TV and movies, it seems that electronic media have somehow taken over our children's lives. Yet kids, when given the opportunity to use their imaginations, will play for hours with small figures. Parents who are willing to interact with their child will learn a lot about him. Kids can choose such things as cowboys and Indians, sea and land animals, pirates and swords, miniature family members, cops and robbers, ambulances and fire trucks, trees, wizards, monsters, volcanoes, household furniture, babies, doctors, nurses and band-aids, treasure chests and booty, or dishes and silverware. They will use their imagination to come up with all kinds of themes, arrangements and interactive activities on their own, if you let them.

As with puppets, parents can sit on the floor with their child and participate. Watch how your child plays with the toys. Is she gentle and kind or rough and harsh? What kinds of situations does he make up? Does he create hiding places, fight scenes or prefer to play games of escape? After watching for a while, ask your child what role he wants you to take. If your child has been suffering from overwhelm, watch to see if she incorporates any of the elements of the event (divorce, accident, molestation, hospital visit, disaster, etc.). When kids make various play scenes with objects, creating with their imagination and their hands, something magical happens to relieve their stress and tension. The important thing is that children get to express and expel the energy bound up in their emotions. This is how they are able to come back into balance and retain a sense of self.

For preschoolers, a sand box in the backyard can provide a place to sit in and play with both small and large objects. This type of play involves both the sensory experience of touching the sand and the motor experience of manipulating toys and figures with small fingers. It is a marvelous vehicle for working out problems. As with children's drawings or other forms of therapeutic play, what is most important is the child's experience of having her world, her feelings and her creativity witnessed by a caring adult. A child feels safe when parents refrain from judgments or advice. Connection takes place without words when there is an acknowledgment of the "hands knowing how." As Carl Jung wrote, "Often the hands know how to solve a riddle with which the intellect has wrestled in vain."[2] The adult's job is to step inside their child's experience in order to connect with him at an emotional level.

Dramatic Play/Dress-Up and Role-Play

Dramatic play, like puppet play, gives children the necessary psychological distance from their problems, creating safety to express their thoughts and feelings unabashedly. This type of play is both natural and spontaneous. It's the easiest way that children have to communicate with each other and with parents who are willing to connect with their world through play.

In her wonderful new book, *Hidden Treasures: A Map to the Child's Inner Self,* Violet Oaklander tells the story of an adopted ten-year-old hyperactive boy with explosive anger, despite medication.[3] Joey had been found tightly tied with rope to the seat of an abandoned car when he was five years old. This boy clearly needed to be in contact with a safe adult who could set the conditions for him to experience a sense of power, control and escape.

After several sessions of building the relationship through contact-enhancing shared activities, this boy spotted a set of handcuffs on the toy shelf. He then took control by setting the stage. He assigned Violet the role of robber, designating himself as policeman. Joey had her pretend to steal a wallet so that he could come after her and catch her. He played this game with great enthusiasm. During the second session of this same play theme, Joey expressed the wish for some rope to tie her up. Violet brought in rope the following week, continuing this type of play. He went through the sequence of chasing, grabbing, putting her in handcuffs and tying her up several more times until he tired of it. This freed him up to create different play themes that were less reminiscent of his early trauma. Soon after that his mother reported "that he was a transformed child—happy, no longer destructive, calm."

Like Joey, other children who have experienced frightening situations where they felt trapped, pinned down, attacked or in any other way out of control need to have active restorative experiences. An added benefit in this type of energetic play is that it evokes muscles involved with defensive postures and movements.

In turn, this is likely to restore a sense of strength and competence that may have been lost during overwhelm. When children engage in make-believe play, self-consciousness disappears. One empowering activity to help children develop healthy defenses is to invite them to pretend to be their favorite animals. They should be encouraged to take on the characteristics and motor movements of those animals. They can growl, hop, jump, bare their teeth, spring, rattle, claw, swim, slither, pounce and hiss.

Although it is not necessary (keeping it simple is sometimes best), children can have fun elaborating on this type of play by making their own animal, people or fantasy masks out of cardboard or papier maché. As they hide behind these masks, they can more easily connect with their own inner power as they act to express feelings. They might be confronting a fire-breathing dragon while actively dodging the flames, running fast to safety or practicing a slow-motion soft landing on pillows or rubber mats. Other themes might be finding a safe place to hide, winning a sword fight or battle, playing doctor or nurse as they stitch up a cut or pretend to drive a car as they twist and turn the steering wheel to avoid an accident. With dramatic play, as with puppets and toy figures, children are engaged in physical activity that creates the opposite sensations and feelings to those of helplessness and immobility.

Art Activities: Clay, Play Dough, Painting and Drawing

Clay and Play Dough

Clay and play dough are wonderfully tactile. This soft material can be molded and re-molded. Figures can be made and then smashed and re-made. Because of its malleability, as kids feel and shape the bits and pieces it reinforces how things change. Kids can make shapes or fashion figures. If your child is able to form tiny clay people, you might even encourage her to talk to the clay models, saying anything and everything that she may not have the courage to express in person. She can even fashion loved ones that are no longer with her due to death, divorce or abandonment. Young children (or older ones for that matter) can simply make a lump and pound on it, triumphantly wielding power over whatever it is that the lump represents.

Finger-Painting and Drawing

Sensory experiences help children to build a strong sense of self. Finger-painting is a great way for kids to express their emotions and resolve their difficulties. It's almost as if an understanding of their deep feelings emerges from their tactile and gooey creations. We have used finger-painting successfully with hyperactive children. Some have become amazingly calm and attentive to their projects and report feeling better afterwards even though they were not able to describe their upset with words. It can also be a wonderful bonding experience to paint quietly side by side with your child. Sometimes your child might invite you to join with her in creating a painting together.

For kids old enough to draw, the following activities can help your child to sort out and work through his feelings. Ask your child to tell you about the scene he sketched. Look for signs of both the traumatic incident and evidence of resilience and restoration in your child's drawings. Refrain from giving advice, making interpretations or judging what has been portrayed. Instead, ask about how she imagines the various animals or people in her sketch might be feeling. If there are objects, you might ask her to tell a little bit more about the objects and their relationship to the other figures. Notice if your child puts herself in the picture. If not, ask if she ever feels the way she imagines any of the characters feel in her scene. In other words, the key is to look at your child's drawing with an attitude of openness and curiosity. This will allow you to connect with your child's inner world, rather than superimposing your notions and emotions.

Free Form

Give your child drawing paper and felt-tip markers in assorted colors. Ask him to pick a color to make some doodles (squiggly lines) to show how he feels right now. If he wants to talk about his drawing and/or feelings, listen attentively. If not, don't push him. Ask him to draw some more doodles using different colors as his moods change.

Sensation Body Maps

If your child is preschool through third-grade age, have her lie down on butcher paper while you trace her entire body with a marking pen. Help her to make a coding key to describe sensations and emotions that she feels, using a variety of colors and/or markings. Kids are instructed to color and mark different places on their body map where they feel different sensations and emotions using their own personal key.

Examples of coding keys are:

- Blue = sad
- Orange squiggly lines = nervous
- Pink polka dots = happy
- Black = numb
- Purple curvy lines = energetic
- Red = hot and mad
- Brown = tight

Kids seven years and older can make a "gingerbread" person shape on a large sheet of paper. Have your child draw his own coding key in the margin. Next, he fills in the body map to indicate the location of any sensations and emotions he is feeling in the moment. Be sure to encourage the expression of both comfortable and uncomfortable feelings.

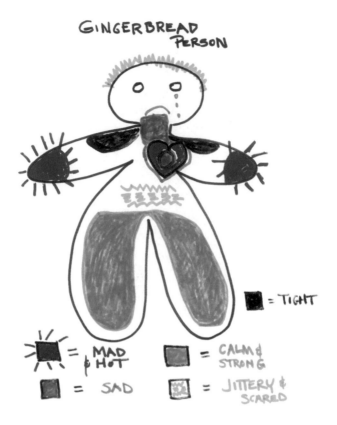

Variation

For kids who are very young, very shy or learning-delayed, the sensation body map can be modified. To keep it simple, have your child choose only two colors for her coding key: one color for comfortable feelings (ones she likes) and the other for uncomfortable feelings (ones she doesn't like). The outline of the gingerbread person can be drawn by the parent.

Drawing a Scene or Story to Show What Happened

Have your child draw something that illustrates what happened to her. Rather than give specific instructions, tell her to make her picture any way she wants. Children often will put in fantasy creatures such as angels, ghosts of cherished relatives and pets or superheroes that help them to work through their trauma. Remember that your child's drawing is neither for the purpose of art nor accuracy. In the context of healing traumatic stress, kids' sketches are for the release of pent-up energy that leads to transformation. Artistic activity is a safe way to explore and understand feelings. Anything goes. Artistic freedom often brings emotional freedom.

Drawings of Worries and Fears, and their Opposite

If drawing the incident does not bring your child a sense of relief, the structured drawing exercise below can be a great help in fostering a change of mood:

Have your child make two drawings on two separate sheets of paper. One drawing depicts a worry, fear or whatever prevents him from feeling good; the other drawing shows the opposite—something that brings a feeling of comfort, hope, goodness, happiness, safety or ease. Often children will do this naturally; they draw a disaster like a car crash and afterwards draw a rainbow. It doesn't matter which drawing comes first; allow your child to decide. When finished, kids can share with their parents the sensations and emotions they feel when they look at each drawing, one at a time. After the sharing is finished, your child can cover his "worry" drawing with its opposite and notice how his sensations and feelings change. A modification of this is to have him fold the art paper in half, using one sheet instead of two.

Drawing Pictures of Resources That Help Kids Cope

Everybody has resources. It can also be said that *every* body has resources. They include whatever supports and assists physical, emotional, mental and spiritual well-being. They can be external, internal or both. Children are born with internal resources but are dependent on adults (an external resource) to mirror and nurture them so the resources will become tangible. In this way, a child can call upon her own reserves when needed. The best resource of all is for a child to be able to feel inner strength and resilience after a stressful event has pulled the rug out from under her.

External resources can aid a child to regain confidence and fortify him internally. These help children to cope in troubling times. (Examples include pets, grandparents, planting a garden, a friend's house, a favorite auntie, poems, singing, playing ball, making things, swimming, mom or dad, stuffed animals, writing letters, playing outdoors, siblings, teacher, God, collecting rocks, biking, scouts, hiking, drawing, reading, dancing, playing the oboe, soccer team, dancing, the mountains, the beach, their room, praying, doing math, gymnastics, playing pretend, looking at the stars, grandma's feather quilt, paint set, chemistry set, baking cookies, skipping stones, talking to friends, playing tag, etc.)

After exploring resources with your child, have her choose and draw a picture of something that helps her cope. Next, have her recall the most recent time she was with the person or pet or did the activity she selected, and notice how it makes her feel inside (emotions and sensations). To deepen this experience, have her close her eyes in order to better describe and locate in what part of her body she feels the sensations. Younger kids can point to the places inside that feel good.

Nature and Animal Rhymes Combined with Drawings That Build Resources

Simple poems such as the ones below or others that you make up with your child can be a delightful way to support healing. The nature verses on the following pages were designed specifically to help kids from approximately three to eleven years of age build empowering resources. They may, however, appeal to youngsters slightly older or younger and can be adapted in any way that suits your own child. Different verses are crafted for different reasons. Some have animals because kids love them. The animal antics shown here can help your child rediscover strengths that may have been lost ... or, perhaps, that she didn't know she had. Your child can draw illustrations to go with the verses that reflect her own resilience and strength.

[Note: The drawings shown here were contributed by Juliana DoValle, then age eleven.]

A rationale for each set of verses is presented beforehand; suggestions on how to help your child get the most out of them follow. Enjoy!

How to Use the Rhymes That Follow

1. Read the verses silently first.

2. Read the notes that follow with ideas about how to use the verses interactively with your child to get optimum results.

3. Read the verses to your child slowly, observing any responses.

4. Taking cues from your child, try the exercise suggested. Take the time to help him feel and work his sensations through or to discuss his responses and questions.

5. **Proceed s-l-o-w-l-y!** For some children you might read as little as one paragraph a day if appropriate. The important thing is to use the rhymes as a starting point, utilizing only what is relevant for your child's age, stage of development and situation.

The first verse, "The Magic in Me,"[4] will help your child connect with his own body through the grounding and centering exercise that follows.

Note: These rhymes are read aloud in *It Won't Hurt Forever: Guiding Your Children through Trauma.* This CD audio series by Sounds True is a recommended companion to this book. The complete set of rhymes with illustrations is also available in the authors' first children's book, *Trauma Through A Child's Eyes: Awakening the Ordinary Miracle of Healing, Infancy through Adolescence,* North Atlantic Books, 2007.

"The Magic in Me" Tree Exercise

We're going to play, but before we begin,
I want you to find your own magic within.
Just take some time to feel and to see
All the great things that your body can be.
Pretend you're a tree with your branches so high
That you can reach up and tickle the sky.
What's it like to be strong like a big old oak tree?
With roots in your feet and your leaves waving free?

Suggestion: After reading the above verses to your child, pause here to give him time to explore what his body can do. Ask him to stand up tall and pretend that he is a "big old oak tree" or his favorite tree, if he has one. Give him sufficient time to stomp and explore his connection with the ground. He can pretend that he has long roots growing out the bottom of his feet deep into Mother Earth. Ask him to tell you how it feels to have roots that go so deep into the ground.

After your child explores her connection to the ground, have her pretend that the wind is blowing through her "leaves" and "branches." Encourage her to hold her arms way up high, swaying to and fro to find her center. Next have her move her arms, feeling her resilience like the graceful bamboo. You might have her bend her "branches" from side to side, noticing how close to the ground she can get before she loses her balance. Have her find her center of balance again and again.

The verses continue:

> Or you can be like a river that flows clean and free . . .
> From high in the mountains right down to the sea.
> Your breath can flow through you, just like a river
> From your head to your toes, feel yourself quiver!
> Now you're connected to the earth and the sky,
> It may make you laugh, it may make you cry.
> It doesn't matter when you go with the flow . . .
> Your branches up high, and your roots way down low.
> Hear the breath in your body, if you listen it sings,
> Now you are ready for whatever life brings!

Suggestion: You might play music of various tempos. Children can experience different paces and rhythms, imagining gentle breezes and tropical storms. After modeling a few different movements, encourage your child to create her own. Make sure that your child's feet are making good contact with the ground by having her place her soles and heels flat on the floor, rather than standing on her toes. If your child needs extra support, you can bring her awareness to the lower legs, ankles and feet by lightly pressing down on the tops of her feet with your hands until there is good contact with the ground. The Tree Exercise is fun to do outdoors on the grass when the weather permits. Be sure to have fun together!

Escape Drawings

Escape is a universal antidote for helplessness. Every child should feel competent in being able to access the desire to run freely. This exercise will help build a child's confidence in their ability to identify and escape from scary situations.

Once your child feels grounded you might want to try this drawing activity: Ask your child to share how he managed to find safety after a challenging event. Or you might ask how he escaped or knew that things were okay again. Did someone help him or was he alone? Was he able to do anything to help himself? How did he signal grown-ups that he needed help?

Have your child focus on one or two elements:

1. What action your child took to escape or find safety. (Examples: moved to higher ground, made herself look bigger so she could be seen, made herself smaller so she wouldn't be seen, walked, ran, hid, climbed, pushed, stood up on her tippy toes, cried for help, froze, shouted, kept quiet, held his breath, made a plan, called 911, waited, prayed, crawled, reached out, held on, pulled away, ducked, covered her head.)

2. Who or what helped her. (Examples: a sibling, neighbor, her ability to kick, scream or run, rescue worker, tree limb, belief in a higher power, a pet, Red Cross, luck, time, medical staff, inner strength, rope, his ability to keep quiet and still, a friend, turning quickly, paramedics, life vest, a parent, her agility.)

Now have your child draw and color his "escape scene." Afterwards, have him look carefully at his drawing and find the part that brings him a feeling he likes. (Examples: powerful, strong, lucky, comforted, loved, supported, warm, brave, proud, fast or clever.) Finally, have your child locate the internal sensations that accompany these feelings. Allow plenty of time for him to savor them. As he does this, have him notice if the good feelings spread to other parts of his body.

Rhymes and Drawings That Bring Feelings of Strength

The next set of verses provides children with the resources of power and strength. Children need to feel confident to defend themselves (like they couldn't do during overwhelm) in order to transform trauma into a positive experience. In the following poem, Rapid T. Rabbit will help children engage their innate "flight" resources, which will kindle the power, exhilaration and the crucial energy discharge of a successful escape from danger.

How Fast Can You Run?

Charlie Coyote is ready for lunch
Being quite clever, he follows a hunch
He crouches down quietly in the tall grass
Then patiently waits for a rabbit to pass.

Rapid T. Rabbit bounds down the trail
She stops to eat clover, then washes her tail
Up jumps coyote, he makes a great leap
Hoping to catch Rapid Rabbit asleep.

Rapid moves quickly, with a jig and a jog
With a zig and a zag, then she hides in a log.
Coyote is clever, Coyote is tough
Coyote is fast, but not fast enough.

Have YOU ever had to run fast and escape?
*Can you feel your LEGS, their **strength** and their*
   shape*?*
You have a body that's healthy and strong.
You can jump high and you can jump long.

*Feel the **power** in your arms, they swing as you run*
*Feel the **b·e·a·t** of your HEART and the **warmth** of*
   the sun.
*Feel the **b r e e z e** on your face; does it tickle your hair?*
Feel your HANDS and your KNEES as you fly through
   the air.

*Now you have come to a **safe** hiding place*
*Take a **deep breath** because you won the race!*

How does it feel in your TUMMY and CHEST
Now that you've found a safe place to rest?

Pay attention to all the movement within
How does it feel right after you win?
Be aware of your breath, it comes in then goes out,
When you feel great, you might even shout!

Suggestion: The verses above can be used to deepen awareness of two important elements to overcome trauma—the bodily sensations of *escape* and *safety*. In the first part of this rhyme, allow time for your child to deepen the sense of power as he feels the instinctual forces of running and jumping (and any others that may emerge, such as ducking, twisting, kicking, "zigging" and "zagging"). Have him pretend that he is the rabbit as he zigs and zags, running to safety.

When kids associate movement with strength and the power to avoid threat, they develop self-esteem that comes from their core. This builds the kind of confidence that remains even when children are under stress because it has become an automatic "motor memory," like riding a bicycle. To deepen this memory, after your child has had time to run and explore her strength, have her draw and color an action picture that shows her in motion. If she is too young to illustrate a movement, have her draw colorful squiggly lines that show how the actions feel.

In the second part of this rhyme, your child gets the chance to pause to experience what it feels like to be safe inside his body. This rhyme continues with a further exploration of the location of sensations of safety:

Do you feel the tingling and the warm energy?
Where do you feel it … can you show it to me?
When you feel glad, you're full of happiness
Can you tell me, inside you, where your
*   happiness is?*

Drawing a Safe Place

Invite your child to close his eyes and rest comfortably in either a sitting or lying-down position. Take the time to help him relax by asking him to bring awareness to the rhythm of his breathing and having him find places in his body that feel calm and places that might be tight or tense. Ask him to see what happens if he takes a deep breath and exhales slowly, making the sound Haaaaaaaaaaah once or twice before returning to normal breathing. When he seems sufficiently relaxed, have him imagine a special place where he feels completely safe. This place might remind him of a spot he already knows, or it can be totally made up from his imagination. What's important is that your child creates this place exactly as he wishes. He can add stuffed animals or real pets; it can have bean-bag chairs or soft shaggy rugs and blankets. It can have over-stuffed chairs and pillows. Your child can be alone, with aliens or have people who love him in the scene. Photos, posters and art-work can be on the walls. He can have pets and plants or friends (real or imaginary).

After your child has had sufficient time to create her space, have her explore it as if she were walking around inside of it. Next have her find a comfortable place to relax in her space. If she can't find a comfortable space, invite her to make one up as a fantasy. Once she's done this, ask her to notice what sensations arise that let her know that she is safe, and have her describe exactly where in her body she knows this to be true. Finally, after taking time to explore the sensations of safety, have her draw and color a picture of her "safe place."

Creating Movement and Change When Fearful Feelings Are Stuck

If, after taking the time to create and explore a safe place and to describe feelings, your child is stuck feeling fearful, have him tell you what worries him. Have him show you where he feels scared and where he feels safer inside himself. He can also draw one pic-ture of himself feeling happy and safe and another of himself feel-ing frightened. If the fear takes more room than the safety, find ways to help your child feel safer and spend time developing "islands of safety" inside. This can be done by reminding her of a time she felt safe, showing a photo of a favorite family member she feels safe with, giving her a favorite toy or stuffed animal, hold-ing, rocking and hugging or any safe touch that your child responds to in a positive way. You can also have her "build" her own hiding place with pillows and sheets or cardboard boxes and play hiding games.

The last part of this rhyme also helps move sensations that are "stuck" in discomfort. These verses give specific suggestions for what your child can do if this happens:

If you pay attention to the places you point to and name
Does it change how they feel, or do they stay the same?
*If they stay they same, here's what **you** can **do***
*To help the stuck feelings **move** right out of you.*

[You might even close your eyes for a minute or two.]

See if there's a color or shape you can name,
As you watch it closely, it becomes like a game.
Your feelings may move from place to place.
***Watch** the fear go without leaving a trace.*

Imagine that you're at your favorite place,
It's quiet and safe in your own special space.
Who would you like to be there with you?
Your mother, your father, or Winnie the Pooh?

Your brother, your sister, your dog, or your cat?
Or perhaps Dr. Seuss, with his cat in the hat.
Would you like to be held by someone, just right?
You can R E L A X and breathe easy as they hold
*   you tight!*

Or, would you like to have someone close by
*Just in case you get **MAD**; or you need a good cry.*
Sometimes crying can make you feel better,
It's just like laughing, only it's wetter!

Suggestion: To help children release uncomfortable feelings that seem to stay stuck, such as a pain in the tummy or a feeling of heaviness in the chest, use the verses (along with the following suggestions) for releasing the sensations. With eyes open or closed, have your child focus on the sensations for a minute or two. Gently ask if the "knot," "owie," "pain," "rock" or whatever they are experiencing has a size, shape, color or weight. Allow sufficient time between questions for your child to quietly feel and process images and sensations. Next, guide him to the present moment by asking how the "owie" feels now. Continue, proceeding slowly, until you notice the "stuck energy" beginning to open up by closely observing your child's body language for subtle shifts (especially more relaxed breathing and posture), as well as listening to her words.

Toward the end of this section of verses, where the rhyme asks kids who or what they want with them, take the answers seriously. Take some time to validate your child's wishes and explore his emotions. Allow time to assess and support any needs that come up, especially to help reinforce a sense of safety and security by being a good container for any tears, anger, sadness or fears that may arise. This simply means calmly listening and acknowledging that you are present for whatever he is feeling. Your job is not to "fix" your child's feelings but to give your undivided attention so that he can feel what's real for him, and can process feelings so the sensations and emotions move forward on their own as nature intended.

Past, Present and Future Drawing

Another activity to keep your child from being stuck in the past is the drawing exercise below, designed to give your child a sense of the movement of time. It can also assess how your child might perceive her future. Have her fold a large sheet of drawing paper into thirds so that the folds are vertical. Direct her to label PAST at the bottom of the first column or fold, PRESENT at the bottom of the middle column, and FUTURE at the bottom of the last column. Then have her draw three pictures in the appropriate columns to represent her life as it was, is now, and how she predicts it will be in the future.

This drawing can be adapted for younger children. Simply explain that "past" means what happened before the bad thing, "present" means how they are feeling and coping now, and "future" means what tomorrow may be like. You may need to fold the paper and print the words for them.

If a child's future looks grim and is similar to the past, work with his here-and-now feelings from the drawing that depicts the present. Ask what sensations he is aware of as he looks at the drawing. Guide him to focus on the sensations and watch how they change. If he feels unpleasant sensations, help him to track these until there is a discharge using the suggestions above for releasing discomfort. When your child begins to feel more pleasant (or at least tolerable) sensations, have her check to see if her perception of the future has changed. If it is changing for the better, have her draw a new FUTURE picture on another sheet of paper. As she looks at her latest creation, have her notice and track the new, more pleasant sensations and feelings that may be emerging. Exercise caution in pushing her to feel better before she is ready; allow time for feelings to transform organically. The more you are tuned-in, the more you will be able to follow (like the trail left by brother and sister in the fairy tale of Hansel and Gretel) the "bread crumbs" that your child is dropping in the dark forest to help you help them find their way back home (to themselves).

CHAPTER IV

Remedies for Specific Situations: Amusement Park Rides to Zebra Bites

It is commonly believed that trauma is caused by catastrophic events or long-term abuse. While it is certainly true that these events leave humans vulnerable to trauma, symptoms are not a result of the event itself but of how a particular situation is perceived, assimilated and processed by one's nervous system. Therefore, with effective emotional first aid even after horrific events such as Hurricane Katrina, war, 9/11 and the Indian Ocean tsunami, children's acute stress reactions do not automatically lead to chronic stress disorders.

At the same time, a simple tumble off the sofa, ride in the car during a fender bender or routine medical procedure is capable of setting up a nasty series of long-term symptoms or a loss of resilience. This is not because the happening was horrible but because your child's developing nervous system was overwhelmed with fear. Without first aid, this fright may get strongly imprinted, causing a disturbance in the child's ability to withstand ordinary stress. Over time multiple problems might arise. These can range from a lack of self-confidence and low frustration tolerance to serious anxiety and other mood and behavioral disorders, such as Attention Deficit Hyperactivity Disorder (ADHD).

Fortunately, there is so much that you as parents can do to help your child maintain confidence, joy and resilience . . . even after a mishap! This chapter will guide you in helping with the inevitable accidents, falls and medical procedures that are part of any child's ordinary life experience. You will be guided in preparing your child for surgery to reduce the risk of traumatic reactions. This chapter will also give you timely tips on how to bully-proof your kids. Although this chapter on first aid highlights only the aforementioned potential sources of distress, the information and skills you learn here can be applied to an entire alphabet of ailments which include these and more: **A**musement park rides, **B**ullies, **C**rashes, **D**ental work, **E**levator rides, **F**alls, **G**unshots, **H**igh-chair tumbles, **I**noculations, **J**ellyfish stings, **K**ickball injuries, **L**ost at the mall, **M**edical procedures, **N**ose dives, **O**perations, **P**ossessions lost, **Q**uarrels, **R**oller skating slip, **S**titches, **T**onsillectomies, **U**mbrella pokes, **V**olcanic eruptions, **W**itnessing violence, **X**-ray machines, **Y**our choice and **Z**ebra bites.

First Aid for Accidents and Falls

Accidents and falls are probably the most commonplace source of potential trauma. They are a natural part of growing up. In fact, as infants turn into toddlers, they must fall in order to learn to walk. It is actually the sense of moving from equilibrium to disequilibrium and back to equilibrium that spurs growth. Although falling and accidents are unavoidable nuisances, living with trauma symptoms afterwards can easily be avoided. Remember, too, that what may appear insignificant to an adult can be shocking to a child even though there is no physical injury. Also, a child can easily keep their feelings hidden if they believe that "not being hurt" or "being a big girl or big boy" who doesn't cry will keep parents from getting upset.

Of course, most falls are not overwhelming. When the body first senses that it is off balance, it tends to do a bit of acrobatics to prevent what could be a painful landing. Especially when there is no injury or scare, minor mishaps are a gift in that they provide the opportunity for any child to enhance her sensory awareness and practice "first aid" as she builds resiliency as a kind of "stress inoculation" for whatever life brings. However, sometimes the landings are hard, even very hard, and may cause a substantial fear reaction.

The "First Aid for Accidents and Falls" guide below will appear somewhat familiar, as it overlaps with the basics that you learned in Chapter II. The "old" material will serve as a review of the "nuts and bolts" of trauma prevention, no matter what the event, while the new material pertains specifically to accidents and falls. The following guidelines can be used whatever your perception of the severity of the mishap. Beyond a doubt, an ounce of prevention is worth a pound of cure.

Eight-Step First Aid Guidelines

1. Attend to your responses first.
(This step, as outlined in Chapter II, cannot be overemphasized!)

Take time to notice your own level of fear or concern. Next, take a full deep breath, and as you exhale slowly sense the feelings in your own body until you are settled enough to respond calmly. An overly emotional or smothering adult may frighten the child as much, or more, as the fall or accident itself. Remember the analogy of "putting your own oxygen mask on first" when sitting next to a child on the plane.

2. Keep your child still and quiet.
If safety concerns or the nature of the injuries require that the child be picked up or moved, make sure that he is supported properly. Carry your child—do not allow him to move on his own, even though he may be able to. Remember that he is probably in shock and does not realize the extent of the injury. Because the child's body is likely to be surging with adrenaline, this might be difficult. Use a firm, confident voice with a ring of authority that conveys in a loving manner that you are in charge of protecting him and know exactly what to do. Keep your child comfortably warm by draping a sweater or blanket over his shoulders and torso. If there is the possibility of a head injury, do not allow him to sleep until your doctor gives the "OK."

3. Encourage plenty of time for safety and rest.

This is particularly true if your child shows signs of shock (glazed eyes, pale skin, rapid or shallow breathing, disorientation, overly emotional or overly flat expression or acting like nothing has happened). Do not allow him to jump up and return to play. Help your child know what to do by modeling a relaxed, quiet and still demeanor. You might say something like, "After a fall, it's important to sit (or lie) still and wait until the shock wears off. Mommy's not leaving your side until that happens." A calm, confident voice communicates to your child that you know what's best.

4. Hold your child.

If your child is an infant or very young, you will probably be holding him. Be sure to do so in a firm but gentle, non-restrictive way. Avoid clutching tightly, as well as excessive patting or rocking, as it might interrupt recovery by interfering with natural bodily responses. To communicate support and reassurance to an older child without disturbing the process, it is suggested that you place your hand on her back just behind her heart, or on the side of her upper arm near the shoulder. A warm, "healing hand" can help your child to feel grounded as *your* calmness is directly communicated through touch. This is, of course, if your child is receptive to being touched.

5. As the shock wears off, guide your child's attention to his sensations. (Steps 5 and 6 serve as a review from Chapter II and are at the heart of preventing and healing trauma.)

The language of recovery is the language of the instinctual brain— which is the language of sensations, of time and of patience. Just as touch is important, so too is your tone. Softly ask your child how he feels "in his body." Repeat his answer as a question—"You feel okay in your body?"—and wait for a nod or other response. Be more specific with the next question: "How do you feel in your tummy (head, arm, leg, etc.)?" If he mentions a distinct sensation, gently ask about its location, size, shape, "color" or "weight." Don't worry about what these sensations *mean;* the important thing is that the child is able to notice and share them. Keep guiding your child to stay in the present moment with questions such as "How does the rock (sharpness, lump, "owie," sting) feel *now?*" If she is too young or too startled to talk, have her point to where it hurts.

6. Allow one or two minutes of silence between questions.

This may be the hardest part for parents, but it's the most important part for your child. This allows any physiological cycle that may be moving through your child's system to release the excess energy and move toward completion. Be alert for cues that let you know a cycle has finished. These cues include a deep, relaxed spontaneous breath, the cessation of crying or trembling, a stretch, a yawn, color coming back into the face, a smile, orienting to her surroundings or the making of eye contact. Wait to see if another cycle begins or if there is a sense it's time to stop. Keep in mind that there is a lot happening in your child's nervous system that may be invisible to you. That is why waiting for a sign that things have shifted is so important.

7. Do not stir up discussion about the accident or fall during initial first aid.

It is best to not talk about the mishap by asking questions to alleviate your own anxiety or curiosity. The reason for this is that the "story" can disrupt the rest period needed for discharging the excess energy that was aroused. Telling about it can wind kids up just when they need to be settling down. It is in the quiet waiting that the involuntary sensations such as shaking, trembling and chills begin the cycle that soon leads to calm relaxation.

After the releases happen, your child may want to tell a story about it, draw a picture or play it through. If a lot of energy was mobilized, the release will continue. The next cycle may be too subtle for you to notice, but rest (rather than more talk or play) promotes a fuller recovery, allowing the body to gently vibrate, give off heat, exhibit skin color changes, etc., as the nervous system returns to equilibrium.

These changes happen naturally. All a parent has to do is provide a calm, quiet environment and a few focused questions to gently guide the process. It can be challenging to provide a tranquil space when family members gather around asking, "What happened?" In response, you might simply and politely say, "Not now ... we'll talk about it later after your sister rests a while." Talking about the details of the accident to your child (or in front of your child) can aggravate an already activated nervous system, adding an additional layer of unnecessary fear. This can abort the healing process! If siblings want to express their care, they can follow your lead by saying something calming, such as "Stay real still so you can be good as new soon" or "It's okay to cry, little brother. It can make you feel better." Please refrain from shaming statements, such as "I told you that you'd get hurt playing on those stairs!" Also, refrain from judgmental statements, such as "You are such a clumsy kid!"

8. Continue to validate your child's physical responses.

Resist the temptation to stop your child's tears or trembling. But keep contact with her, reminding her that whatever has happened *is over* and she will soon be okay. In order to return to equilibrium, your child's discharge needs to continue until it stops on its own. This part usually takes from one to several minutes. Studies have shown that children who are able to cry and tremble after an accident have fewer problems recovering from it.[1]

Your job is to use a calm voice and reassuring hand to let your child know that "It's good to let the scary stuff shake right out of you." The key is to avoid interrupting or distracting your child, holding her too tightly or moving too far away.

How Long Does It Take?

With minor tumbles, accidents and scares, the steps outlined above may be all that is needed. This relatively easy eight-step First Aid Guide for Accidents and Falls can be followed right on the spot where the calamity occurred. For example, if your child has twisted an ankle while skating on the front sidewalk, grab some ice and a blanket and minister to him at the site of the fall (if safe). The steps can take anywhere from five to twenty minutes as the physiological cycles complete. It's not unusual for the trembling to start after the blanket and ice are applied as the child feels tended, warm and safe. Teeth may begin to chatter after a few minutes of rest and/or tears of release may begin to roll down the cheeks before a sigh of relief completes a cycle.

When the fall or accident creates a medical emergency, the first aid steps can be used by a parent while in the car or ambulance on the way to the hospital. Once your child discharges some of the excess energy, you can prepare her for what to expect at the emergency room or doctor's office. Choose your words wisely when preparing her for the medical procedure. Use simplicity and honesty framed in a way that will benefit her. You can do this by using positive suggestions. For example, if your child needs stitches, let him know that they will sting but will make the "owie" heal faster and better. Discuss and practice what you will do to focus attention away from the pain. For example, have him squeeze your arm and imagine that with every squeeze special "cream" makes the pain float away like a balloon. See "The Power of Language to Soothe and Heal" in this chapter for more on timing and choosing words wisely.

The Purpose of Touch When Helping a Child in Shock

While paying close attention to a child's bodily responses, you will be most effective in supporting reactions as they emerge by taking special care when giving physical support. A parent's touch can either help or interrupt the normal cycle for coming out of shock, depending on how the touch is applied. If you are caring for an infant or young child, hold him safely on your lap. If it's an older child, you can place one hand on her shoulder, arm or middle of her back. Physical proximity of a caring adult can help a child feel more secure. Be mindful, however, not to hold your child too tightly as this will interfere with the natural discharge that will follow. The focus of intention when touching a child is to convey:

- Safety and warmth so your child knows she is not alone;

- Connection to your grounded and centered adult presence;

- Confidence that you have the ability to help him surrender to his sensations, emotions and involuntary reactions as he moves toward release and relief by not interrupting his process due to your own fears;

- Trust in your child's innate wisdom that allows her body to release as she moves toward resolution and recovery as her own person and at her own pace.

Your body language is more important than knowing the exact words to say. Because we are social creatures, we read each other's clues to figure out the seriousness of a situation, especially in an emergency. Your children not only read your expression but rely on it for their sense of safety. Translated into practical terms, this means that the look on the parent's face and shown by your posture can foster either safety or terror.

You want to minimize unnecessary upset with your own wide-eyed expression, because what you really want is to be a steady anchor. Become mindful of your own involuntary responses. Practice brings poise. Opportunities in modern life abound to practice first aid on your own self. For example, after a near collision in your car, pull over to a safe place and track your sensations until you feel a sense of relief and completion. This can also be done after witnessing violence, or experiencing a fall, injury, shocking news or other stressful event. You can even practice during a scary movie.

The Power of Language to Soothe and Heal

When something dramatic happens out of the blue, it can put a person in an altered state in which they are particularly susceptible to suggestions from those around them. And, of course, with medical procedures that require anesthesia, children are purposely put into an altered state. Skillfully selected words and the timing and tone of voice with which you use them have the power to speed recovery. This is true whatever the nature of the frightening event.

In *The Worst Is Over: What to Say When Every Moment Counts* by Acosta and Prager, the authors give numerous examples of verbal first aid that salvaged seemingly hopeless situations, stopped serious bleeding and even prevented scar tissue from forming in burn victims![2] We know how easy it is for words to either put us at ease or make us tense. Words can turn an ordinary experience into a romantic one, raise or lower blood pressure and bring either laughter and joy or tears and sorrow.

The following list is a useful framework for choosing words wisely. Use your tone of voice to convey to your child that you understand what it must feel like to be in her shoes. Then say something that accomplishes the following:

- Shows your child that you compassionately accept what happened.

- Ensures that your child feels safe and connected, rather than alone.

- Reassures him that whatever happened is over (if it is).

- Helps "move time ahead" from the past to the present by guiding him to notice sensations until there is a discharge and shift.

- Reminds him of his resources to help him cope. (Read Chapter III to review resources.)

When an accident occurs, recount to your child what happened to him in simple, honest language that he will understand. For example, after a fall resulting in a small cut with heavy bleeding, you might simply say something like this: "That fall really took you by surprise, huh? That tiny cut sure is bleeding! Let's clean it up real good. I'll hold a cool cloth on it to stop the bleeding and make it feel better. Then you can pick your favorite colored band-aid. I know just what to do so you'll be good as new. You can help put it on if you'd like." (Or, to an older child, "You can even put the band-aid on yourself, if you'd like that.")

Then, after the immediacy of the injury has been tended, look for bodily clues such as pale skin, cold sweaty palms, shallow breathing and wide eyes. Your child is probably still somewhat stunned so it's best for her to be sitting or lying down. Then you might say something like, "The hard part's over; your cut is healing already! But honey, you're still a bit shook up ... Daddy will stay right here with you until the (shaky or numb, etc.) feeling wears off. You might get a little shivery or jittery or wiggly ... or maybe even a little giggly. It could be that some more tears will come. I'll stay with you (or you can sit on my lap) until the very last tear (or jitter or shiver) is gone. Then we can make up a silly story (or draw a picture if your child enjoys this more) about what happened to share later with Mommy."

EXERCISE: EXPERIENCING THE POWER OF WORDS

Not only are words powerful at the time they are spoken, in times of openness and vulnerability they become etched in our memory. Take a moment now to recall words that have shaped the peaks and valleys of your life, and you will have an experiential understanding of just how penetrating they are and how they have textured your life.

Part A

1. Write a paragraph or two using all of your senses to describe everything you can remember about a kind person who used words, touch, gestures and/or actions to comfort and soothe you after something bad happened. Recall in as much detail as possible what it was that they said and did that made you feel better and recover.

   Find a comfortable place to rest. Recalling what you just wrote, notice how you are feeling in your body now. Take some time to focus on sensations, emotions, thoughts and images. Notice what happens to your body's expression and posture as you sink into the experience in this moment. Notice which sensations let you know that this memory was a pleasurable one!

   It's possible that when you did this exercise, an unpleasant experience may have surfaced as well. That's because the amygdala, the part of the brain that imprints emotional memories, stores strong surprise encounters as well. Intense experiences are registered, whether they are pleasant or unpleasant.

   Because of these imprints, it may be that you recalled insensitive treatment when what you *really* needed was to be nurtured by an understanding adult. This can be especially hurtful when it was a parent or other close family member who wasn't able to comprehend what you were going through. If this was the case, you can do the following exercise in order to have a different experience now. As you heal your own wounds, you are less likely to react to your child blindly by repeating your familiar pattern. Perhaps that is exactly why you are reading this book!

Part B

1. Write a paragraph or two using all of your senses to describe everything you can remember about an insensitive or unaware person who used words, touch, gestures and/or actions that made things worse instead of soothing you after something terrible happened.

2. Without dwelling on the unpleasant experience that you just described, allow an "opposite" image to help transform any images, words, sensations and/or feelings that you might have recalled. Try not to censure what pops up. Allow the *newly formed opposite scene* to expand, providing as many healing details as possible. What words, touch, gestures and actions are bringing you relief? What in particular is comforting you, making you feel better and soothing any wounds from the past? Allow yourself to hear the words and see the actions *now* that you needed back then—replay it *in this moment* in the same way you would hope to nurture your own child.

3. Find a comfortable place to rest. Recalling your new and restorative image, notice how you are feeling in your body. Take some time to focus on sensations, emotions, thoughts and images. Notice what happens to your body's expression and posture as you sink into the experience now. Note what sensations let you know that this new memory, using your adult resources, is affirming or pleasurable!

Addressing the Emotions through Listening and Storytelling

In more serious or complex situations, your child may have lingering emotional responses that need tending. Children and adults alike often feel embarrassed or awkward after an accident or fall, especially if it was in front of peers. They may feel shame or guilt, especially if the accident caused damage to property, clothing or special possessions. They may have these same feelings because of medical or other expenses that were incurred that might burden the family financially.

After you have completed giving emotional first aid and your child is rested and calm, set aside some time to discuss feelings about what she experienced. This can be done later that day, the next day or whenever new emotions emerge. In addition to shame and guilt, children often feel anger, sadness and fear. Help your child to know that those feelings are normal. Listen carefully and reflect back what was said so that your child is sure that you heard and understood. *Refrain from trying to fix or change her feelings.* Trust that feelings change by themselves when parents or other supportive adults can "hang out" with a child in this zone of uneasiness. This kind of support not only makes the temporary discomfort tolerable; it improves the ability of children to withstand frustration without falling apart.

Working Directly with Accidents and Falls When Symptoms Are Present

When working with falls, big soft pillows can be helpful in giving a child the opportunity to practice falling safely. Have your child stand in the middle, surrounded by pillows, and calmly kneel beside him or her. Place your hands gently (but firmly) on your child's neck, shoulders, lower back or in any configuration that will allow you to control their fall. With your hands to support your child securely, gently guide a slow fall, pausing if he seems to stiffen or startle. You can let your child know that you're going to play a "rocking and rolling" game. It's often best to start with your child sitting and gently rock him from side to side and then forward and backward. Make it fun by letting her rock *you* back and forth also, letting yourself go off center and back to center as a model. You can both roll around a little on the pillows (forward, backwards and sideways). Then she can "fall," a little at a time, into your supporting arms and onto the pillows.

This type of "play," which involves a guided fall with a safe landing, helps to develop good protective reflexes and restores confidence. Recovering from a fall involves re-establishing innate equilibrium responses. A child-size fitness ball can be used to practice going from balance to off-balance and returning to balance. (These balls can be purchased at any discount department store.) Again, use soft pillows on the floor around the ball so there is a safe landing. Have your child start with her eyes open and feet spread apart to form a solid base. Gently rock your child from side to side on the ball and see what emerges. Notice if your child reflexively uses her arms, legs and torso to protect herself or if she depends on you to catch her. If she's somewhat tense and rigid, invite her to imagine how her body might respond if you weren't next to her. Continue to explore and practice until she is able to engage her reflexes. As your child becomes more relaxed and proficient, parents can up the challenge by having their child close her eyes the next time. Once there is a sense of falling, all parts of the body prepare to prevent the fall. When prevention is not possible the arms, elbows, wrists, hands, knees, legs, ankles and feet end up in all types of configurations in an attempt to buffer the impact. Don't be surprised if you see the whole "ballet" sequence that happened when your child took his tumble, performed in slow motion through this type of "pillow play" as you catch your child from a free fall.

If your child needs more distance from the fall because the fear is too intense, you can begin by using a doll or favorite stuffed animal to create a scene similar to your child's real-life experience. An example would be: Babar the elephant falls backwards out of the high chair. Refer back to the story of Sammy in Chapter III to guide you in this type of play. As your child role-plays, be sure to watch his responses closely. *Always leave him with a sense that he can succeed*, giving him only as much support as he needs. Gradually introduce the idea of him taking turns with the stuffed animal and/or with you or his siblings, friends or parents.

More Animal Rhymes to Help Your Child Regain Self-Confidence

If your child's fall has been extremely shocking, perhaps even compounded with an injury that required a trip to the emergency room, it may take more time, patience and approaches to help your child come completely out of the "freeze" or "shut-down" response. The best way to restore your child's confidence is to go slowly with a pace that will encourage opening up rather than closing down even more. Just like the nature and animal verses in Chapter III helped your child to feel grounded, powerful and safe, the following poems were designed to help remove any shame, shyness or self-doubt that your child might be carrying about having been too scared to protect or defend herself. Let your child know that our animal friends have the same kinds of responses we do.

In the next set of verses, Oscar Opossum demonstrates that the "freezing response" (or "playing possum") is a very important survival mechanism. When children can't fight, run or avoid accidents and falls, this response protects them. This instinctive behavior is, unfortunately, often judged by both adults and kids to be cowardly or weak. The Oscar Opossum rhymes demonstrate to your child that the "freeze" behavior is not only normal, but, oftentimes, the smartest choice possible.

When youngsters listen to the story of how Oscar outwits Charlie Coyote by pretending to be dead, two things will be accomplished. First, the "freezing response" will be seen as positive and empowering; second, the identification with the opossum's ability to come out of his frozen state without fear of his own bodily reactions can help your child move through her own frozen states without fear or shame. This understanding can lead to better feelings about herself when she's experiencing these helpless and troubling involuntary states. It is also reassuring to realize that with a little time and patience those feelings give way to a "letting go" that may be shaky at first but soon leads to relief and, perhaps, even a smile!

In the rhyme below, Oscar Opossum shows children how he temporarily freezes to protect himself. When the "coast is clear," Oscar easily comes out of this natural protective state by simply shaking and trembling away all the "boiling energy" he was holding inside.

Oscar Opossum

Oscar Opossum is **slow as molasses**
He plods right along, while everyone passes
When he sees coyote, he **can't run**, *so instead*
He rolls up in a ball and **pretends that he's dead!**

Oscar **escapes**, *you see, by* **lying quite still**
Not *like the rabbit who* **runs** *up the hill!*
Oscar has all his energy **BOILING** *inside*
From holding his breath to pretend that he died.

*Can you **pretend** that you're Oscar rolled up in a ball?*
*You're **barely breathing**, and you feel very small.*
It's cold and it's lonely as you hold on tight
Hoping coyote will not take a bite!

Suggestion: Pretend with your child that both of you are being chased by something bigger and faster than you. Ask your child who he wants to "chase" him. It might be a tiger, bear, other beast or monster. Stop running and, instead, roll up in a tight ball, holding as still and quiet as possible to "trick" the beast into passing you by because you are so well hidden or look like you've died! Take time to explore sensations without talking and hold still for as long as you can so that there is a sense of release and relief when you finally let go, get your breath back and let all your muscles relax.

The verses continue with questions to help explore normal emotional responses that may arise before and after coming out of the "freeze response."

Do you remember ever feeling this way?
You wanted to run, but you had to stay.
Were you SCARED, were you **sad***, did it make you*
   MAD*?*
Can you tell what you felt to your mom or your dad?

Suggestion: Children may "open up" with their true feelings and thoughts after you read the above verses. Allow sufficient time for them to share. Pause, observe and listen to your child carefully, showing that you care about any and all emotional expressions that may emerge. After acknowledging your child's feelings, making it safe for him by refraining from judging or fixing; you might help him explore more deeply. Ask open-ended questions, such as "What else do you feel?" or use statements such as "Tell Daddy what else about that scared you." Or simply, "Tell Mommy more."

The Charlie Coyote and Oscar Opossum verses continue:

You Don't Have To Be Afraid

Oscar Opossum has to lie low
But **inside** *his body, he's ready to blow.*
When Charlie Coyote finally takes off
Oscar Opossum **gets up** *and* **shakes off***.*

See Oscar **tremble***, see Oscar* **shake**
Just like the ground in a little earthquake.
After he trembles and shakes for a while
He feels **good as new***, and walks off with a SMILE!*

Coyote has gone, now **get up** *and run [whisper]*
But **first** *you might* **tremble** *and* **shake** *in the sun.*
Before long you can jump, you can skip, you can stomp
Or play in the meadow and have a good romp.

Feel the blood flow through your HEART and
     your CHEST
Now you are safe and now you can rest!

Suggestion: Have your child pretend to shake and tremble, first exaggerating the movements by dramatizing them. After some fun active movement, have her lie down and rest, noticing the energy and flow inside her body. This will help her to feel more subtle sensations that will most likely be pleasant and warm.

The next set of verses, "Bowl of Jell-O," is silly and intended to playfully expand children's awareness of their inner landscape of sensations in order to help them prepare for a discharge.

Bowl of Jell-O

Can you pretend you're a big bowl of Jell-O?
Red, purple, green, or even bright yellow?
Now make-believe someone gives you a jiggle
And you start to shake and tremble and wiggle!

As your fingers tremble, feel your heart pound,
Now feel the shaking go down to the ground,
Feel the trembling in your arms, the warmth
     in your chest,
Don't try too hard; you're doing your best.

In your belly and legs, feel the vibration,
Let it flow like a river, it's a pleasant sensation!
Feel the energy move from your head to your toes,
Feel the strength in your body, as the good feeling
     grows.

Suggestion: Continue by making up your own verses (together with your child if she is old enough), appropriate to her situation and needs. Verses like the ones above can help children experience bodily sensations without becoming unduly frightened. Through

this heightened body awareness, the discharge of energy necessary to return to a normal state can occur safely and playfully.

Tips for Working with Automobile Accidents

When a child has been involved in any kind of accident, you may
eventually need to reintroduce (and "desensitize") her to the ordinary objects and experiences that remain "charged." The child's
behavior when the offending object or experience is seen or mentioned will let you know which elements of the accident bring up
painful or overwhelming reminders. Sometimes the connection is
obvious; at other times it is not.

Sometimes the "charge" doesn't develop into full-blown symptoms until the period of shock and denial has worn off. This often
can take weeks. The main idea is to introduce the "activators"
slowly so as not to overwhelm your child further. The following
example of working with an automobile accident can be adapted
for a variety of ages and situations.

After an automobile accident, the infant's or toddler's car seat
could be brought into the living room. Holding the infant in your
arms, or gently walking with your toddler, gradually move toward
it together and eventually place the child in the seat. The key here
is to take baby steps, watching and waiting for responses such as
stiffening, turning away, holding the breath or heart rate changes.
With each gentle approach toward the avoided or fear-provoking
encounter, the same step-by-step procedure outlined in steps four
through eight at the beginning of this chapter can be used as a
guide. The idea is to make sure that your pacing is in tune with
your child's needs so that not too much energy or emotion is
released at once. You can tell if the latter is occurring if your child
seems to be getting more "wound up." If this happens, calm her
by offering gentle reassurance, touching, holding or rocking. Stop
if she shows signs of fatigue. The whole sequence does not need
to be done at once!

Rhymes to Help Kids after Sports Accidents

Once you have connected with your child in such a way that you are certain she feels understood, she will most likely be more receptive to your inspiration and guidance. It is at this point that sharing a similar experience that you or someone you know has had might be helpful. Another idea is to make up stories and verses like the ones provided in this book. For example, "The Story of Dory," below, is about a girl who had a bad fall from her bicycle and became overwhelmed. One way to use this story is as a starting point or model for you and your child to make up one of your own. Customize verses to your particular child's age, needs and situation. Another way to use the story below (and others like it) is as an "assessment" tool. Parents can use stories and drawings to consider whether a particular situation has left lingering distress. Read "The Story of Dory" aloud slowly while carefully watching your child's reactions, as well as noticing what he has to say. Do his eyes widen like saucers? Does his body stiffen? Does he say, "I don't like this story" and try to slam the book closed? Or does he get "squirrely" and agitated? If your child identifies with some of Dory's reactions to the fall, the likelihood is that he has had a similar experience and relates to her feelings. When you observe a reaction, stop the story and help your child experience the sensations and emotions that he is struggling with by being present as a calm, non-judgmental witness until the uncomfortable emotional expression begins to change to relief.

After reading the story, you can have your child illustrate it and make up a picture story of his or her own (as a young friend of ours did for this book). If children are too young to draw a picture, have them scribble to indicate how they feel. Provide an assortment of colored crayons or markers and model for them how to make different lines, such as squiggles, circles, jagged, wavy and straight. They will automatically draw in a way that reflects their feelings.

The Story of Dory

Sit back, relax, and I'll tell you a story.
The hero, my friend, is a girl named Dory.
She plays first base on her Little League team,
To have a new bike was her favorite dream.

On her last birthday, this girl's dream came true.
She got a new bike that was bright shiny blue.
She jumped on the bike and rode down the block,
Faster and faster, then the bike hit a rock.

She felt the wheels skid, and she flew off the seat,
And then she landed real hard on the street.
She hit the pavement with a big thud,
Then she saw that her knees were covered with blood.

She started to cry, but the sound wouldn't come,
She couldn't breathe, and her body went numb.
When she noticed the blood on her knees,
Like Oscar Opossum, she started to freeze.

Later that day Dory felt bad.
She also felt sad, and then very mad.
On her new bike things had happened so fast
That she could do nothing at all, except crash.

It wasn't her fault, but she took the blame,
When she thought of her bike, Dory felt shame.
If something like this ever happens to you,
Can you tell mom and dad what you might do?

Suggestion: Take time to discuss with your child how she might deal with a similar situation. Remind her of the lessons learned earlier from our animal friends, Charlie Coyote and Oscar Opossum, and the importance of letting the sensations and feelings move freely through the body.

After you shake, you can jump, you can run,
You can hide like a rabbit or play in the sun.
You can kick, you can cry, you can laugh, you can feel,
You can dance, you can sing, or do a cartwheel!

A Guide to Constructing a Healing Story

Earlier in this chapter, you were given step-by-step guidance to help prevent traumatic symptoms immediately after an event. Frequently this is all that is needed. However, when the event was particularly threatening to your child, symptoms may develop despite your best efforts. Stories and drawings are especially useful when a child's upset continues after you have given "trauma first aid."

When using stories, generally the adult needs to tell the story of what happened (from the adult's perspective). The next step is to invite your child to add to this story or tell his version. A child who at first is reluctant to talk will usually be glad to chime in to "correct" his mom or dad with his version by saying, "No, that's not what happened; —————— is what really happened!" Be sure to look for certain universal elements that need to be addressed whenever your child is overwhelmed. You can find those crucial elements in the example of Dory above. They include:

- The excitement before the accident
  (Verses: "On her last birthday, this girl's dream came true" and "She jumped on the bike and rode down the block.")

- The scary parts before the actual impact (where energy is mobilized)
  (Verses: "Faster and faster," "hit a rock," "wheels skid," and "flew off the seat.")

- The actual impact of the accident
  (Verses: "landed real hard" and "hit the pavement with a thud.")

- The resulting physical injury (if there is one) and horror
  (Verses: "her knees were covered with blood.")

- The freeze response
  (Verses: "the sound wouldn't come," "she couldn't breathe," "her body went numb," and "like Oscar Opossum, she started to freeze.")

- The emergence of mixed emotions
  (Verses: "Dory felt bad. She also felt sad, and then very mad.")

- The emergence of inevitable guilt and shame
  (Verses: "she took the blame" and "Dory felt shame.")

- The discharge of activation from overwhelming
  sensations and emotions
  (Verses: "you can shake, you can jump, you can run, you
  can kick, you can cry, you can laugh, you can feel.")

- The resolution of traumatic activation with a successful
  outcome
  (Verses: "You can dance, you can sing or do a
  cartwheel!")

Adults are frequently puzzled by intense reactions that appear disproportionate to the nature of the event. It is important for you to take your child's reactions seriously. Often children are communicating lingering upset from an earlier unresolved incident that has been re-stimulated. Take the opportunity to work it through. This is more likely when the recent event stirs up reminders of a situation in which your child was more vulnerable due to age and/or the severity of the earlier mishap. The body records and remembers everything from infancy and toddlerhood. Conscious memory may be lacking since preverbal experiences have no narrative. You may be surprised at what guilt, shame or worries emerge from these stories and from the artwork your child makes to illustrate them.

More on Working with Stories

Sometimes, especially with very young children, it is best to use a make-believe child, animal or doll as a substitute for your own child in the story. This may initially help to give needed distance from the event to make it less frightening. In the tale be sure to include some of the scary stuff one element at a time. For example, if your child fell down the stairs, if it's not too disturbing, add in the part about the stairs if your child leaves it out. Observe your child closely to see if he identifies with the reactions and feelings that the make-believe character in the story has. Stop the story to help your child work through any sensations and emotions that get triggered. If she gets anxious, follow the same steps as recommended for first aid. For example, have her point to where she feels the scary feelings and ask her to tell what "color," size or "shape" they are. Remind your child that you will stay with him as his sensations and images change their quality, shape and size and finally disappear! Insert any of the elements listed above that are missing and seem to be essential for resolution of the trauma.

Prevention of Medical Trauma

The Importance of Preparation When Medical Procedures Are Necessary

One common and frequently overlooked source of trauma in children is routine and emergency medical procedures. Armed with the knowledge you will acquire in this section, ideally you can work together as a team with clinic and hospital staff. This joint effort can greatly reduce unnecessary overwhelm for your child from invasive medical and surgical procedures. But before we introduce you to the strategies, first read the surprising story that follows:

TEDDY

"Daddy, daddy, let it go, let it go! Please don't kill it! Let it go!"

These are the terrified screams uttered by ten-year-old Teddy as he bolts from the room like a frightened jackrabbit. Puzzled, his father holds a motionless tree shrew in the palm of his hand, one that he found in the back yard and brought to his son. He thought it an excellent and scientific way to teach Teddy how animals "play possum" in order to survive. Startled by the boy's reaction to his seemingly harmless gesture, Teddy's father is unaware of the connection that his son has just made to a long-forgotten event.

On Teddy's fifth birthday the family pediatrician and lifelong friend came for a visit. The whole clan gathered around the doctor as he proudly showed them a photograph he had taken at the local hospital of baby Teddy at age nine months. The boy took a brief look at the picture and then ran wildly from the room, screaming in rage and terror. How many parents have witnessed similar mysterious reactions in their children?

At nine months of age, Teddy developed a severe rash that covered his whole body. He was taken to the local hospital and strapped down to a pediatric examination table. While being poked and prodded by a team of specialists, the immobilized child screamed in terror under the glaring lights. Following the examination he was placed in isolation for seven days. When his mother, who had not been allowed to see him for over a week, arrived at the hospital to bring him home, Teddy did not recognize her. She claims that her son never again connected with her or any other family member. He did not bond with other children, grew increasingly isolated and began living in a world of his own. Though by no means the only factor, the hospital trauma experienced by nine-month-old Teddy was an important, possibly critical, component in the shaping of Theodore Kaczynski, the convicted "Unabomber," who sent letter bombs to various people involved in technology and wielding corporate power—arguably, his revenge against the same dehumanizing forces that overwhelmed and broke him as an infant.

The Hospital Experience as a Possible Source of Trauma

Without appropriate support, children do not have the inner resources to comprehend the blinding lights, physical restraints, surgical instruments, masked monsters speaking in garbled language and drug-induced altered states of consciousness. Nor are they able to make sense of waking up alone in a recovery room to the eerie tones of electronic monitoring equipment, the random visitations of strangers and possibly moans of pain coming from a bed across the room. For infants and young children, events such as these can be as terrifying and traumatizing as being abducted and tortured by revolting alien giants. Ted Kaczynski's "crusade" (though utterly misguided) against dehumanization by technology begins to make more sense when we learn about his traumatic hospital ordeal as an infant. This systematic and sociopathic murderer thought deeply about the ideology behind targeting corporate offenders (and left reams of writing behind in his wilderness shack), yet his unsuspecting letter-bomb victims were mere cogs in the same dehumanizing machine. It was a futile, and randomly harmful, gesture of impotent rage. It is the type of tortured adult behavior now being correlated with multiple childhood traumas, such as medical injuries coupled with separation or abandonment by parents. (You can read more about the relationship between antisocial behavior and multiple childhood traumas throughout *Ghosts from the Nursery: Tracing the Roots of Violence* by Robin Karr-Morse and Meredith W. Wiley, New York: The Atlantic Monthly Press, 1997.)

Unfortunately, this story is not an isolated incident. All too many parents have witnessed the disconnection, isolation, despair and bizarre behavior of their children following hospitalization and surgery. The evidence suggests that these long-term behavioral changes are connected to traumatic reactions to "routine" medical procedures. But, is this possible? The answer is yes.

Does this theory imply that if your child has been traumatized by a medical procedure, he will go berserk or become a serial killer? Not likely. Most traumatized children do not become criminally insane. Instead, events like these become internalized in a process we call "acting in," which may later show up as anxiety, inability to concentrate or aches and pains. Or the past events may be "acted out" as hyperactivity or aggressiveness. In this regard, let's look at a more "ordinary" story from the pages of the American magazine *Reader's Digest,* entitled "Everything is Not Okay," where a father describes his son Robbie's "minor" knee surgery:

> The doctor tells me that everything is okay. The knee is fine, but everything is not okay for the boy waking up in a drug-induced nightmare, thrashing around on his hospital bed— a sweet boy who never hurt anybody, staring out from his anesthetic haze with the eyes of a wild animal, striking the nurse, screaming, "Am I alive?" and forcing me to grab his arms. . . . Staring right into my eyes and not knowing who I am.

Tragically, stories like this are commonplace, often leading to the formation of avoidable psychic scars. In 1944, Dr. David Levy presented extensive evidence that children in hospitals for routine reasons often experience the same "nightmarish" symptoms as "shell-shocked" soldiers.[3] Sixty years later, our medical establishment is just beginning to recognize and acknowledge this vital information. What can be done to reverse the tide of unnecessary medical trauma that harms millions of children annually?

Fortunately you do not have to wait for our medical care system to change. If the frustrated father of the boy with knee surgery had known what you are about to learn next, he could have helped prevent his son's terror brought about by his overwhelming hospital experience. Traumatized children can have nightmares, become hyperactive, fearful, clinging, withdrawn, bed-wetters or impulsively aggressive or even violent bullies in the aftermath of medical procedures handled insensitively. Others are beset with chronic headaches, upset tummies or depression. When concern for children's emotional safety is minimized (or worse, ignored altogether), there is a huge price to pay.

What Parents Can Do to Prepare Children
for Surgery or Other Medical Procedures

All kids want a parent to be with them during treatment. According to a *U.S. News and World Report* cover story in June 2000, that is one point on which all experts can agree. Yet there is a good deal of apprehension among these same experts regarding the advantage of having parents present. Medical personnel frequently don't want parents to be partners on the team—and for good reason. An emotional, demanding parent would interfere with safety and efficiency, to say nothing about upsetting the child.

In the magazine article cited above, Leora Kuttner, a psychologist who studies pain in children at British Columbia's Children's Hospital in Vancouver, tells of working tirelessly with a youngster about to receive a spinal tap, but she was unable to distract him from his fear of pain. Knowing how important it was for him to relax in order to prevent a terrible treatment, she continued to try. After exhausting every technique without success, she glanced around, only to discover the sideshow that was happening behind her! This is what the psychologist reported: "Behind my back was Mom, sobbing, sabotaging everything, sending the message, 'My darling, what are they doing to you?' Her fear got in the way, and she undermined what help could be given to her child."[4]

Your presence can be helpful, but only if you are not visibly anxious yourself! During the procedure the parent needs to reassure and comfort—at times, even distract—the child. If you feel like you are going to break down in tears, you may instill fear and tears in your child. *During the procedure* this is not what is needed! (Even though, as we have seen, right *after the child is injured and before medical procedures are begun,* crying can allow the child to discharge fear and shock.)

For medical personnel, the idea of having a parent in the room may be new, may go against typical medical school training and at first glance may appear counter-productive. However, if you remain calm with a helpful presence, the staff is more likely to allow you to push the limits a bit in terms of how much you can be with your child. It is important to educate not dictate! When you select a clinic or hospital that allows you, the parent, to work as a team for the emotional well-being of your child undergoing various procedures, the pay-off can be enormous. In addition, the reputation of the medical facility will grow when the statistics begin to show improved recovery time and patient satisfaction. A shortened hospital stay and speedy recuperation cut costs for the health care and insurance companies. It's a win-win situation for all the parties involved.

Since it is not uncommon for children to be traumatized by surgeries and other medical interventions, concrete recommendations for parents are outlined below in hopes that their adoption will ameliorate this potentially devastating situation. *Three procedures that can be particularly terrifying to a child are: 1) being strapped down to an examining table (especially in an already frightened state), 2) being put under anesthesia without being properly prepared for what to expect and 3) waking up in the recovery room either with masked and "monstrous" strangers or alone.* Parents can do quite a bit to help children feel more comfortable through careful groundwork. These "readiness" steps are likely to greatly reduce the inclination for your child to panic.

The organized activities listed below will support you, the parents, in becoming proactive. They are the "meat" of medical trauma prevention. Once you know what's best to help your child, you can talk knowledgeably to the doctors or nurses responsible for your child's care. The recommendations are arranged according to what you and your doctor can do *before, during* and *after* the medical procedure or surgery.

Before the Day of Surgery

1. Choose a doctor and hospital that are exquisitely sensitive to children's needs. Not all doctors and facilities are created

equal! Take the time to "shop around." Find a doctor who uses kindness, playfulness, distraction and honesty to work *with* your child when she is fussy or resistant, not against her! You can tell by the pediatrician's words and actions whether he or she is able to alleviate your child's worries rather than compound them.

Look for a hospital that has social workers to help kids. Some even have specially designed programs using story and role-play with children to prepare them for what to expect. In some of these programs even the youngest children get to meet the surgeon or anesthesiologist in the role-play room. Doctors are not always aware of these programs, so investigate on your own and find a user-friendly team that will listen to what you have to say and adopt a patient-centered approach. Remember, you are the consumer!

2. Prepare your child for what will happen. Tell him the truth without unnecessary details. Children do better when they know what to expect; they do not like medical surprises. If you tell them it won't hurt when, in fact, it will hurt, you have betrayed their trust. They will come to fear the worst when they cannot rely on you to be honest. Children and teens undergoing surgeries have been observed to be remarkably less frightened at hospitals with a staff that orients them to each and every step.

3. Staff and parents can arrange a time beforehand so your child can meet with the doctors (especially the surgeon and anesthesiologist) in their *ordinary clothes* before they are dressed in surgical garb and mask. It is important for your child to see that the doctor is a human being who will be helping him, not some monster from outer space! Perhaps your youngster can even put on a doctor's costume too. If that's not possible, he can put a disposable surgical mask on himself, a doll or favorite stuffed animal.

4. If the hospital does not have a program to prepare children, or even if it does, you can have your child dress up in a gown to play "hospital." Children can dress puppets, dolls or stuffed animals in medical attire and play "operation" at home, going through all the steps in advance. These include riding on a gurney, getting injections and preparing for anesthesia. Have a dress rehearsal. Most toy stores have play figures and "medical kits" for children, complete with stethoscopes and injection "needles."

5. Prepare your child both *emotionally* and *physically* for anesthesia by practicing entering into and coming out of an altered state. First, you can prepare him emotionally by making up a story similar to what your child's experience might be like. An example would go something like this:

   When Hibernating Bear is in his surgical gown, Nurse Nancy Bear puts a mask on his face or gives him a "special tonic" that goes right into the veins on his wrist (or gives him a cup of brew or some pills) to make him go to sleep *very, very quickly* so that he sleeps right through his operation. That way he doesn't feel anything. When Hibernating Bear wakes up, he feels very, very, strange. It's different from the way he feels at home when he opens his eyes in the morning. It seems like it takes forever to awaken. Very, very slowly Bear comes out of his fogginess and grogginess. Then he looks for Momma or Poppa Bear or Nurse Nancy Bear and something good to eat! (Obviously the parents need to check with the anesthesiologist to find out exactly how their child will be sedated. They also have to make sure that arrangements have been approved for them to be in the recovery room when their child wakes up if this is possible; if not, they need to know who will be there with their child as she comes out from under the effects of anesthesia.)

   For older children, parents can use favorite characters

from fiction, such as Harry Potter. Harry might get the "magic-potion injection" that puts him to sleep so he can recover with speed from the terrible whopping he received by the Slytherins. Or you can use fairytale characters such as Sleeping Beauty. Whatever you use, make sure that *your* child relates to the character and that you have fun together with the fantasy.

Second, help your child prepare for what she can expect to feel physically. Explain that the injection or IV insertion might prick for a second or two. You can ask in advance if numbing cream will be used. If so, you can show your child how and where the balm will be applied and explain that its purpose is to lessen discomfort. It's *especially important* to forewarn your child that the potion or pill may make them feel like they are floating or spinning. You can help your child to practice this feeling by having them lie down and relax deeply by slowly inhaling and exhaling while counting backwards together from five on each exhale. Tell your child to breathe in through her nose, imagining that her lungs are filling up with air like a balloon and then slowly filling all the way down to the top of her belly. Have her exhale every bit of her breath out through her mouth. Once she is calm, have her pretend that she is floating on a cloud and feels as light as a feather. Or, the child can imagine that he is taking a magic carpet ride through the sky in slow motion. If your child likes water, you can have him make-believe he is floating on an air mattress in a pool or on a raft in the ocean.

Another important readiness step in preparing your child for the physical sensations of anesthesia is to get her accustomed to the feeling of dizziness. This can be done by gently and slowly spinning your child around in a circle once or twice (like parents do for piñata and "Pin the Tail on the Donkey" games). Then have her rest, noticing the different sensations that arise. Of if you have a swivel chair, you can spin her around slowly one time to see if she tolerates this feeling. If she doesn't, give her time to settle. Later try a half-spin even more slowly, building up tolerance to this new sensation.

You can also purchase fun spinning toys in most discount department stores. *Spin Around* and *Sit N Spin* are two such toys that a child sits on top of, spinning himself around. The advantage to these is that the child is in control of the speed and number of times that they spin so they can become accustomed at their own pace. Parents still need to be cautious that their child doesn't overdo it and become nauseated in their eagerness to have fun. The idea here is to familiarize children with sensations they might experience at the hospital so that they are not suddenly frightened by the unexpected.

6. Ensure that a local anesthetic is going to be used! Multiple studies have shown that healing from a surgical wound is more rapid, involving far less complications, when local anesthesia has been administered along the line of the actual incision (as opposed to only a general anesthesia that makes one fully unconscious).[5] Unfortunately, this relatively easy-to-do procedure is still not routine, and general anesthesia given without benefit of a local is far more common, even for simple surgeries. If a general anesthesia must be administered for a particular procedure, it is still important that a local be given to your child as well. Doctors and parents together can advocate for medical facilities to adopt such policies. By all means discuss the types and methods with which anesthesia will be given well in advance of the operation date. Of course, if a local anesthetic can be used alone, and your child can be kept from being terrified, then that is generally best.

One of the graduates from our training program carried out a small pilot study at the University of California–San Francisco Medical Center. Her outpatient pediatric rheumatology patients had to undergo an extremely distressing (and repeated) procedure for which they were frequently "put under" because of their terror at having the procedure. Using techniques like the ones just described, she found a dramatic improvement in the children's capacity to undergo the procedure without general anesthesia; and in many cases without much fuss. (See Chapter VIII for more details regarding the work at UCSFMC.)

On the Day of Surgery

1. Parents and medical personnel need to work out an arrangement whereby parents can remain with their child as much as possible before and after the operation. Children do better when a calm parent can be with them during administration of pre-operative drugs. It is also best if parents can get permission to stay until the child transitions from waking consciousness to a "twilight" state.

2. A child should never be strapped down to an examining table or put under anesthesia in a terrified state. This leaves an imprint deep in his psyche and nervous system. The child should be soothed until calmed. Ask the doctor if you can hold him or her. If your child must be strapped down, explain this to the child and remain with her until she is comforted and supported enough to go on. Fear coupled with the inability to move puts a child in a terrified shock reaction—a recipe for trauma!

3. Medical staff and parents need to know that, ideally, parents should be in the post-operative room when their child is waking up. The child should *never* awaken in the "recovery" room alone. Without a familiar adult to comfort them,

many youngsters wake up disoriented and panicked. The state is so altered that they may believe they have died or that something horrific has happened to them. It is important that parents and hospital personnel decide together who will guide the child as she comes to—and be sure to let her know in advance who it will be. If parents are absolutely not allowed, request strongly that there be a nurse or someone else there (whom the child has already met) to make soothing contact when your child awakens. To awaken alone in the post-operative room can be terrifying—even to an adult.

Whoever is with your child can gently re-orient her to the room and to time by letting her know where she is and that the surgery is over. If your child is feeling numb or reports that his body feels weird or is distorted in some way, let him know that this feeling is normal after an operation and reassure him that it won't last forever. It can be very helpful to touch and gently squeeze the muscles on your child's forearm in order for him to get a sense of the boundary of his body again.

After the Surgery Is Over

1. Rest speeds recovery. All of your child's energy needs to be directed toward healing physically. This conservation of energy is important, but children may not understand this. If they want to play, it needs to be quiet play with lots of encouragement to rest.

2. If your child is in pain, have him describe the pain and then find a part of the body that is pain-free, or at least less painful. As you sit with your child, encourage the alternation of awareness between the part that hurts and the part that doesn't hurt so much; this can often alleviate the pain. You can also distract your child a little through the tough

spots by humming with them or having them clap or tap a part of his body. Suggesting that he imagine a variety of colored balloons holding the pain and taking it way up into the sky as they float away can also be useful.

When the Medical Procedure Is an Emergency

1. Once the imminent danger is over—and, for example, you are riding with your child in the ambulance—take the time to observe and assess your own reactions. Allow time to reflect and remind yourself that you now have tools to help; allow time to settle your own shakiness, and wait for your own breath to come before proceeding. A sense of relative calm should be your first task.

2. Reassure your child that everything will be OK, that the doctor knows how to make them better, help them stop bleeding, fix the broken arm, stop the pain, etc.

3. Distracting your child right before the medical procedure can be helpful. Retell her favorite story, bring out her favorite toy or talk about her favorite place, like the park—making plans, perhaps, to go there when she is better. If your child is in pain, you can have him clap, sing or tap himself to lessen the pain. Or you can ask him to tell you a place in his body that feels OK or has less pain, and direct him to focus on that part. Let him know that it's OK to cry.

4. If children are old enough to understand, tell them what will happen at the hospital or doctor's office. For example: "The doctor will sew up the cut so it will stop bleeding." Or: "The nurse will give you either a pill or a needle with medicine to make the pain go away, and that will make you feel better."

A Word about Emergency Rooms

More horror stories have been uncovered from the emergency room experience than from any other area in the hospital. By its nature, there is a frenetic atmosphere. It has been frequently reported to us that although the hospital procedure itself went well, the emergency room was outright frightening and left unforgettable images. Some hospitals have recognized the detrimental nature of exposing children to critically injured adults in the waiting room and treatment area. We encourage your family to visit the local hospitals (urban areas usually have several) before an emergency arises. You may be astonished at the variation in quality of care and nurturance among them. In one large city three local hospitals, within twenty minutes of each other, were visited in doing research for this book. One was totally chaotic and many adults were being treated for domestic violence and gunshot wounds. Another was more or less ordinary, with a pleasant waiting room and the typical long line of patients. The third hospital, refreshingly, was as conscientious about protecting children's psyches as they were about healing their bodies.

To shield the children from the adults, both the waiting and treatment rooms were separate. The children's waiting room had colorful child-pleasing murals on the walls, a big fish tank and no injured adults. Unlike the ward-like atmosphere of the adult treatment room, the children's side had individual rooms to safeguard them from exposure to the frightening sights and sounds of injuries and procedures of their peers. This was not done out of economic motivation; rather, it was done because staff members recognized the importance of sheltering children from unnecessary misery. Unless twenty minutes made a life-or-death difference, which hospital would you take your child to if you knew what was available in your community? Unless your child is delivered in an ambulance, chances are the waiting room time will far exceed the few extra minutes' driving time.

Elective Surgeries

Unnecessary surgeries could easily be the topic of another entire book. Many operations that were once considered "routine," such as tonsillectomies and operations for "lazy eye," have now come into question. Always seek second and third opinions to assess if a surgery is really necessary. Also, without going into depth, suffice it to say that there are two procedures administered routinely due to their purported health benefits that you would be wise to question. These are circumcision and cesarean surgery. Weigh the advantages and disadvantages by reading as much as you can and talking to professionals on both sides: those who advocate and those who discourage the procedure. (If you are planning to have your first baby or more children, you can read about cesarean surgery, circumcision, healthy pre-natal and birthing practices and infant development in our first book, *Trauma Through A Child's Eyes: Awakening the Ordinary Miracle of Healing* published by North Atlantic Books in 2007. Extensive information and further references on these topics can be found in Chapter Ten of that book.)

Sensitivity to Your Child's Pain

As mentioned earlier, remember that all doctors and medical facilities are not created equal. Many pediatricians are so focused on saving lives or on the accuracy of the procedure itself that they lose sight of the vulnerability of the little human being they are treating. The "get-it-over-quick" attitude devoid of sensitive care to the terror and pain that a child is going through must not prevail. Much of this attitude comes out of two common but mistaken beliefs that seem astonishing. One is that infants and young children don't feel or remember pain, and the other belief is that even if they do feel pain, there will be no long-term consequences! For those skeptics, let's take a look at the long-term effects of the surgery experienced by a boy named Jeff.

JEFF

As an adolescent, Jeff gathered dead animals struck by pickup trucks and cars. He brought these animals home, cut open their bellies with a knife, and removed their intestines. At four years of age, Jeff had been hospitalized for a hernia operation. When it was time to put the anesthesia mask on his face, the terrified child fought so hard that the doctors had to strap him to the operating table. Following the surgery, the boy seemed to "snap." He withdrew from family and friends and became awkward, secretive and depressed. Do you remember the story of Teddy at the beginning of this chapter? Just as his hospital trauma was more than likely a critical factor in the shaping of Theodore Kaczynski, the alleged "Unabomber," it is likely that the terrifying hernia operation described above figured significantly in the formative development of Jeffrey Dahmer, the serial killer who tortured, raped, dismembered and ate his victims.

The parents of both these men have spent many anguished hours trying to understand the actions of their sons. They had witnessed the disconnection, isolation, despair and bizarre behavior of their children following hospitalization and surgery.[6] The evidence points to the possibility that these bizarre behavioral changes were connected to traumatic reactions to "routine" medical procedures.

Fortunately a growing number of doctors, nurses and medical centers understand the importance of easing pain at both ends of the age spectrum. Palliative care for our elderly is now being practiced by some. It is the rare pediatrician who would intentionally abuse a child. Yet, the change in mind-set regarding the reality of pain in children was only "discovered" by researchers a little over a decade ago! Doctors actually believed that newborn infants were prevented from feeling pain because of an immature nervous system. It was also thought that young children in general did not remember pain. As a result, babies as old as eighteen months

underwent invasive procedures including surgery without anesthesia (this practice still occurred as late as the mid nineteen-
eighties). Doctors also hesitated to use narcotics on children because
they feared the drugs would cause respiratory problems and
addiction.[7] Little did they understand that addiction is more likely
to come from the disconnection caused by the trauma of cruel
treatment.

What many sensitive parents and professionals may have sus-
pected has now, auspiciously, been given credibility by discover-
ies in developmental science. A *U.S. News & World Report* article
in the year 2000 stated:

> Babies probably get the worst of two worlds: a mature nerv-
> ous system able to feel pain coupled with an immature abil-
> ity to produce neurochemicals that can inhibit pain. And
> even when children cannot remember the actual experience
> of pain, it seems to get permanently recorded at a biologi-
> cal level. Children who received painful bone marrow aspi-
> ration treatments without pain medication, for example,
> suffered more during later procedures even when those were
> done with painkillers, according to a 1998 study in the
> *Archives of Pediatrics & Adolescent Medicine.* "If [pain] is not
> dealt with early, it is worse later," says Charles Berde, a pedi-
> atric anesthesiologist who directs the pain treatment serv-
> ice at Children's Hospital in Boston.[8]

In other words, the initial "pain experience" leaves a deep (traumatic) imprint on the nervous system, which is then re-activated
during later procedures. After reading the first section of this book
on the biological nature of trauma, you probably understand better why children are the most vulnerable to overwhelm due to their
inability to fight or flee. As if that were not enough, medical/sur-
gical procedures are by their very nature the most potentially traumatizing to people of all ages due to the feelings of helplessness
that come from being held down, at the mercy of strangers and in

a sterile room when you are in unprecedented pain! Having to remain still while you are hurting and being hurt is the epitome of the terror of immobility! It is the prescription for trauma! Let us review the simple steps you can take as parents to minimize unnecessary traumatization.

Simple Things Parents Can Do to Ease a Child's Pain

- Be sure to ask for a local anesthetic along the line of incision for surgeries. Some facilities even go so far as to use a spray (Elemax) to numb the site of IV insertion for children. Ask your doctor what will be done to ease your child's pain and request localized relief.

- Use stuffed animals and dolls as props for playing doctor and nurse to help make the sick "puppy" or "baby" or "bear" all better. This is a great way for children to get involved in a distraction from their own pain. It gives them a chance to role-play what will happen to them, and gives the adults a chance to assess the youngster's level of worry in order to give adequate reassurance.

- Older children can be taught relaxation techniques. Audio cassettes in the health section of bookstores and in teacher supply stores have guided instructions to release tension from head to toe. Some use visual imagery as well, such as *Quiet Moments with Greg and Steve* (Los Angeles: Youngheart Records, 1983—www.edact.com), while other recordings use affirmations of well-being during surgery on one side of the tape or CD, with subliminal messages hidden in music on the other. Still others work specifically with breathing techniques combined with systematic tensing and releasing of various muscle groups throughout the body.

- Involve your child's mind in fantasy games and voyages, like taking a magic carpet ride and visualizing leaving the pain behind. This can work wonders. Have her keep adding details to the mental picture to keep her focused on the pleasant image.

- Distractions for the younger child such as blowing bubbles or squeezing a "koosh" ball can alleviate pain.

- Biofeedback is offered in some medical centers. No equipment is necessary if temperature-sensitive "sticky dots" are purchased that change color when skin warms or cools to give a remarkably simple reinforcement for deepening relaxation.

Hooray for Teens with Attitude

A terrific find for teens is a video series produced by the Starbright Foundation that prepares them for what to expect from their hospital experience and how to get the most out of it. This company has even produced a video about the often painful process of re-entry to the trials and tribulations of social and academic life (if the teen's treatment required a prolonged stay, such as with burn victims and children with cystic fibrosis, organ transplants or cancer). This candid, cool, uplifting and empowering series is called *Videos with Attitude* and can be found at www.starbright.org. *"What Am I, Chopped Liver?"* (Starbright 1998) exposes teens to the incivilities of hospital life and lays out their rights and how to communicate with their doctor rather than feeling, as one teen expressed it, "so helpless." Below is a useful summary about the rights of teens. These rights include:

- To be talked to directly by the doctor

- To talk privately with the doctor (yes, this means *without* parents)

- To be told the truth without "sugar-coating"

- To decide what *he* wants to hear and doesn't want to hear
- To be treated as a person, not an object
- To speak her mind
- To ask any and all questions—medical, social, physical
- To question the doctor if he or she is doing something you don't think is right
- To be informed about procedures and what will happen
- To ask questions (and get answers) about side effects of medications, such as if your appearance or ability to participate in sports will change, etc.
- To write a note or have your parents ask the doctor questions if you are too shy
- To let someone know if you are in pain
- To share fears, hopes and other emotions (don't keep things bottled up inside)
- To share his needs and personality so that the doctor knows him as a person
- To change doctors

One common complaint is that the doctor often treats the teen as an object or "case" and fails to introduce himself to the patient, speaking instead to the parents as if the teen weren't even in the room! One girl in the video expressed how much trust she had in the second doctor who "walked past my parents, shook my hand and said, 'OK, I'm gonna get you through this.'"

In *Plastic Eggs or Something? Cracking Hospital Life* (Starbright 1998), teens get to see and hear other teens' impressions of the harsh reality of the glaring lights, hospital attire and other things not-so-fun, such as the food. One teen described hospital life as "a cross between a battlefield and a prison." This hilarious journey through hospital halls prepares teens for what to expect and how to roll with the punches of the unavoidable atrocities. What was the best advice from these adolescents? Make sure to bring a CD player (iPod) and headphones with plenty of your favorite music; bring your own sheets, pillows and clothing if you will be there long term; keep a notepad for questions for the doctor; and "Don't think you're just the receiver at the end. It's YOUR life—be part of the whole process."

A Timely Word about Bullies and School Shootings

It seems like barely a few months pass when we wake up to read the morning paper or hear the news about another ghastly school shooting. Bewildered, frightened and angry, we wonder if this could happen at our child's school; another bullied misfit going crazy and taking out innocent lives along with his own. Fortunately, the statistical probability of something like this happening at a given school is remote. However, what does happen almost any day in any school throughout the world is that children are being bullied.

In fact, bullying is so common that we sometimes make the mistake of assuming that it is normal. And while a certain amount of aggression is normal among children (particularly boys), bullying is not. Although it may not be easy to change bullying in your neighborhood, you can not only help prevent your child from becoming traumatized, you can help "bully-proof" them. What we mean by "bully-proofing" refers to preventing your child from becoming either a perpetrator *or* the victim or both.

We don't know much about why school massacres occur, but we do know a few facts. Although profiles of bullies and shooters vary greatly, what *all* have had in common is that they suffered from anxiety, depression and withdrawal from appropriate peer social activity. And many had been ostracized, made fun of and picked on by kids their own age. We also know that anxiety, depression and withdrawal are often symptoms of unresolved trauma.

It is also well known that children who feel powerless at home will often find an outlet for their rage either with their younger brother or sister, the neighborhood kids or on the school playground. Just like what happens in a domino effect when a boss takes out his fury on an employee—which can cause a stressed bread-winner to then take these frustrations out on the elder children, who in turn might take it out on their younger siblings, who in turn take it out on the family pet—so, too, does a "bully parent" give rise to the birth of a home-grown bully. Schoolyard bullies have often been the victim of abuse or physical punishment. Even without corporal punishment, authoritarian "discipline" that steamrolls over a child's growing developmental needs can spawn a desire to torment others. Kids need to be granted a certain amount of freedom to make choices, decisions and to exert their will, especially in play and when it is safe to do so without causing distress to others.

In the next chapter on ages and stages of development, you will learn that children between the ages of two and four naturally begin to come into their power. Particularly around the age of four, they begin to initiate plans, construct, create and feel their physical prowess. When parents applaud their children's new abilities and skills and give them plenty of "air time," they help to build the kind of solid confidence that deters bullies from invading their children's space. Bullies usually don't approach strong kids with good boundaries; instead, they seem to have special radar that detects the children who are somewhat immobilized and defenseless. Often this is true despite a child's intellectual competence. Nonverbal cues from body language are a dead give-away that a child is filled with shame or is otherwise vulnerable. This, as you already know from reading this book, is often the result of unresolved trauma. By helping your child, through body awareness, to build healthy boundaries, to develop early detection of those who might abuse him and by preventing trauma, you will automatically be "bully-proofing" your child.

It is important to remember that the innocent victims of bullying are kids who are usually anxious and depressed. They often suffer in silence. Although (fortunately) minuscule in number, these rare kids can be the anomalies that eventually explode in a homicidal rage, taking their own life along with that of the other innocents. The more adept a child becomes at suppressing his pain, the more likely he is to blow up. Therefore, it is important as parents to recognize and provide professional help for your child if he continues to suffer silently from shame, depression, anxiety or social withdrawal if your attempts to reach him have been in vain.

Those that do the bullying fare somewhat better. However, although they are outwardly self-confident, they often have fragile egos beneath the surface with a tenuous sense of self, based precariously on their physical strength and ability to intimidate. These children need adults to help them find healthy outlets to express their power in non-violent ways and to develop empathy for others.

A special section, titled "Crisis Relief with Groups," can be found in the last chapter of this book. It was designed to help neighborhoods pull together in the event of a school shooting or any other catastrophe (such as a natural disaster), and to help the adults and children communally cope in the wake of tragedies of such magnitude.

—

CHAPTER V

Ages & Stages:
Building Confidence by Fostering
Healthy Development

When a child has suffered a terrifying experience, it may have a lasting impact on his overall development, even after the terror subsides. It's also possible that the childhood "tasks" of growing up may be stunted even without overwhelming circumstances. Children need adults who understand and provide what is required at each stage of their development. Maturation involves emotional *and* physical well-being.

If parents didn't receive support when they were children, moving from stage to stage, they may feel agitated and insecure as their firstborn grows from a passive infant to the toddler who suddenly runs and climbs, getting into any and everything. They may be at their wits' end as they deal with daily power struggles with their two-, three- and four-year-olds. Or, parents might get flustered watching the "flirtatious" behavior that their five-year-old is exhibiting. And parents of teenagers will get to re-visit any conflicts and issues that were never quite worked through during early childhood.

Parents, equipped with both the knowledge and the emotional maturity to meet their child's developmental needs—while at the same time setting limits—are less likely to raise a child with painful developmental deficits. Being emotionally mature means staying open to recognizing and healing our own early wounds. If your critical needs were not met by your parents, whether due to a lack of skillfulness or outright abuse, you can be guaranteed that your child will push every one of your developmental buttons. When you feel your own temperature rising, either you can be spurred onto a path of personal growth or stumble down one that may lead to family discord or a nervous breakdown! It's your choice. Luckily, the first choice will benefit *both* you and your child.

Responding to Your Infant: Issues of Safety and Trust

How we need to respond to children who have been frightened and overwhelmed depends to a large degree on their age—or more accurately, on their stage of development. Infants are the most delicate and fragile of creatures.

For the first half year of life our children depend on us for just about everything. Without constant ministrations their growth and very survival are compromised. If they are cold, for example, infants can do precious little for themselves. In fact, if the parent doesn't pick the baby up and give warmth by holding him close and swaddling him with a blanket and clothing, the infant could actually die. This is the very reason that their cries are so compelling—they *must* communicate to their caregivers that failure to respond in a timely way could result in death. This is, perhaps, why we feel so out-of-sorts, even desperate, when we fail to successfully soothe our baby. But, as most parents discover (after a bit of nail-biting), they are able to intuit what their infant needs by following their own instincts and impulses. We also learn to, intuitively, differentiate when our baby's distress requires an immediate response, and we wake up in the middle of the night to cater to his needs. It is just this innate sensitivity that ensures our capability to minimize infant trauma, while helping to fortify these tiny beings with a foundation of resilience and security. Our adult nurturing, which instills the essential sense of safety and trust, also bestows a readiness for the next phase of development.

Your Toddler's Needs: "Me Do It Myself"

By the time babies are about nine months old, they are starting to
become autonomous in taking care of their own basic needs. For
example, a newborn cannot turn over if placed on their back or
tummy; they must scream to have a parent pick them up. But a
nine-month-old, by contrast, is able to navigate to some extent on
his own. Not only can he turn over, he can crawl and may even be
able to cruise furniture as he gets ready to take his first independent steps. With this emerging capacity, these older babies begin to
resist being held tightly to the parent's body. Around this time you
see babies stiffen and push against their mom's chest, as though
to say: "Hey mom, don't hold me so tight; give me a little space!"

From this age on throughout the second year of life, our entire
evolutionary lineage drives our body/mind toward separation and
autonomy. For this reason, when two-year-olds take a tumble, they
certainly need comfort and support but not in the same close way
as a six-month-old does. The two-year old needs a little more
"space." This means that parents give toddlers a chance to feel their
own ability to recover balance, equilibrium and dignity, while at
the same time feeling the security of adults they can rely on to help,
only as much as needed. If enough breathing room isn't given for
this to happen, children at this stage of development may feel suf-
focated and are apt to become "terrible twos." On the other hand,
if the parent is distracted and uninvolved during a mishap, the
child at this stage (not yet old enough to have developed strong
self-support) may feel disoriented, overwhelmed or even abandoned.

This knowledge about what children need at different developmental stages is particularly important to keep in mind as you
assist your child during times of stress and trauma. The idea is to
give them enough support to be able to discharge their shock freely,
but not too much physical holding such as clutching or squeezing. This type of overbearing attentiveness can inhibit the spontaneous release of the energy bound up in your toddler's stunned

reactions. It can also inhibit the child's sense of autonomy and confidence in moving through such a distress cycle.

"Tug of War" with Your Three- to Four-Year-Old

By the time children are three or four years old, their capacity to physically engage in the world jumps to new heights. In addition, their facility to delightedly describe their new experiences of the world with seemingly endless stories and artwork begins to blossom. This is the "piss & vinegar" stage of development. Kids of this age are into everything. They are pulling and tugging, pushing and shoving. They are in a perpetual celebration of life. Even more curious than the two-year-old, with the added ability of being more agile, they will pull the dog's tail or auntie's leg just to see what happens. For them, life is a grand, ongoing, "tug-of-war." Not surprisingly, this is the age at which our kids meet—head-on—the unforgiving forces of nature, especially of gravity and momentum. They trip on toys and hit their heads on tables as they run around the house in squealing ecstasy. Rude reminders of the laws of physics—a body in motion tends to stay in motion—are particularly common for this age group when the motion is stopped by a door, or worse, halted by a plate-glass window!

Commonly, kids in this stage of development are said to be "strong-willed." This is because they are learning about power by confronting and overcoming obstacles. Thus the task at this stage is about developing a sense of initiative, power and mastery. However, when kids of this age take their inevitable spills, it feels like having their legs pulled out from under them. When they are overwhelmed, they temporarily lose the very skill that defines them—not only their task, but their very sense of self. If we are frightened, or we shame our kids for their spills, it's all the more dreadful for them.

If the parent is overly protective, the child is doubly wounded: first for the injury itself and second by feeling disempowered and shamed. At the same time, if we just leave her to "stew in her own juices" then she may not regain her equilibrium. To be sure, it is a delicate and dicey balancing act for parents. The trick is to be solidly there for your child with your calm presence. This means standing side-by-side with him and resisting the temptation to scoop him up in your arms and hold him while crying out such things as "poor baby—now look what's happened to you!"

Our kids seem to be without boundaries in their expressions of will and, therefore, do potentially dangerous things such as poking their sister's eyes or sticking their fingers into fans and electric outlets. High-spirited with their tricycles, they delight in racing across the street to their playmate's house. Their exuberance is so great while their sense of danger lags far behind. Children at this stage need parents who set clear limits, that's for sure. And this is where shame comes in. Starting around two years old, shame is what parents (need to) engage in teaching kids what is dangerous and what is safe. It also makes it possible for them to learn what is socially acceptable and what is not.

When you scold your child, something profound happens in their physiology and brain activity. Combined, this makes them feel terrible—in fact, so bad they will not want to repeat the act that they were reprimanded for. It is essential that children get the message at once; their survival may depend on this. However, at the same time you don't want to leave them stuck in shame. When children are regularly scolded, this horrible feeling of shame becomes habitual. There are two killers of vitality and joy; one is fear, the other is shame. The trick here is for the parent to admonish the child for their unacceptable *action* (for what they have done) and *not for who they are*. The way to accomplish this is through words like: "*NO*, you can't ride your tricycle into the street, and you are *never* to do that again ... and Daddy/Mommy loves you to pieces and doesn't want you to get hurt." They must feel your care for them in your tone and body language so that they can recover from the "shaming" experience. This provides a feeling of connection with you that will be more likely to help reinforce the correction you made in your child's behavior.

This is a very different experience for your child than being banished from your sight with the last look he saw on your face implying disgust from an angry, "fed-up" parent. To be able to have the necessary finesse, parents need to take a deep breath and feel their own bodies first, *before* scolding kids. If you stay present within yourselves, then the corrective use of shame will add to your children's growing sense of power, and will and exuberance won't be stifled. This healthy use of shame without damage to the parent-child relationship is a potent weapon against producing a revenge-seeking child in later years.

Another developmental "task" at these tender ages is gender identification. Hence, if children are unduly and chronically shamed during this stage, a tendency may develop into a diffuse shame. This can be reflected in uncomfortable feelings about being a boy or girl, and in becoming a young man or woman later on. Hence, unhealthy toxic shaming can even contribute to gender confusion and deep feelings of being sad and uncomfortable.

Your Flirtatious Four- to Six-Year-Old Boy or Girl

In addition to gender awareness and identification, somewhere between the ages of four and six children feel a special bond and attraction to their opposite-sex parent. This is a normal stage. In fact, this phenomenon is so universal that the Greeks portrayed the unfortunate consequences of this *unresolved* dilemma in the plays *Oedipus Rex* and *Electra*. In popular culture we refer to hopeless romantics who have not detached from this childhood fantasy as having an "Oedipal Complex." (Of course, with new, blended and same-sex households, these stages may show up differently.)

Daughters, especially around the age of five, routinely fall in love with their dads, as do little boys with their moms. Again, this is a normal, healthy stage of development. Kids of this age will "flirt" with the parent of the opposite sex. This is not flirting in the adult sexual sense, but rather a practicing necessary at this stage. In other words, the kinds of behaviors that will later form the repertoire of adolescent peer flirtations are first tested at home where it is supposed to be safe. This is the time when little girls might tell their father, "I love you, Daddy; I want to marry you and have a baby with you when I grow up."

At this delicate, vulnerable age, what is needed to foster healthy development is for the father to tenderly say (and mean) something like: "I love you too, sweetheart, but Daddy's married to Mommy. When you grow up you can marry someone special just for you, and if you want, you can have kids with him. But I'm so glad that you're my little girl and I will always be your Daddy."

Many times, what happens instead is that the child's development may be handled poorly by misreading this truly innocent "practicing" behavior. Instead of the parent helping the child with her emerging sexuality, the response may be more reminiscent of that of a lover, promoting in tone, actions or words their "special" relationship. For example, playful flirtations such as "Yes, my little princess, I'll always be your prince—but let's keep it our little secret," may result in further awkward and inappropriate responses. This "courting" behavior often feels overwhelming to the child and may be frightening to the parent as well. This fear can lead to a squelching of appropriate touch and affection so necessary for emotional maturation.

Well-defined generational boundaries are vital for healthy sexual development. Children are supposed to lose rather than win the Oedipal struggle, with the parents' gentle guidance in accepting reality versus fantasy. They may not like giving up these romantic illusions, but they must! It is better that they accept this disappointment as preschoolers than to grow up romantic fools pursuing partners that are unavailable or worse.

Adolescent Development: Who Am I?

Teenage development, to say the least, can be a very difficult transition for both the teen and his parents. In addition to the emerging social needs of belonging and fitting in to larger groups, two of the earlier stages are re-visited: becoming autonomous (nine months to two and a half years) and seedling sexuality (four to six years), which have been lying more or less dormant during the elementary school years. The newly forming adolescent's separation from her parents with the simultaneous blossoming of sexuality can be downright anxiety-provoking and frustrating for the whole family. Additionally, if these developmental steps were mishandled early on, the teen years can be even more tumultuous.

In the arena of autonomy, the "terrible twos" can come back with a vengeance. The teen who never achieved an initial, albeit immature, sense of self in early childhood may go to extremes of attitudes, risky choices and behaviors in a dramatic attempt to establish distance and distinction. Other adolescents, who were thwarted by early trauma or oversight of their developmental needs, may be too inhibited or shut-down to venture forth into the world, fearfully clinging to and alternately rejecting their parents instead. Lost and confused, both types of youth are vulnerable to substance abuse and promiscuity. They need guidance from their parents during this stage more than ever.

So what can concerned parents do to help their teens? The first step is to recognize and support the need for increasing independence, curiosity and discovery that first appeared in the toddler years. It's never too late to help your child develop a sense of autonomy and mastery. Limits can still be set even though they are more difficult to enforce if they were weak during the toddler stage. Choices and freedom need to be given and expanded as more responsibility is shown by your adolescent. The rules need to be flexible and re-negotiated frequently as your teen matures. It's not so much "laying down the law" as designing agreements that work for both parties. And, of course, the more you are emotionally available to listen to your youngster, the more likely he is to want to earn your trust. Your role is to provide encouragement, safety, choices and guidelines.

For those teens whose formative years did not provide optimum development in the area of healthy sexuality (whether due to sexual violation; separation from the opposite-sex parent due to divorce, military service, death or abandonment; or simply parental awkwardness during the four- to six-year-old stage), there is still a chance to repair gaps in growth. Parents need to be *adults, not peers or buddies* to their teens. Frequently sexual boundaries are weak in adults who were themselves sexually traumatized or undeveloped as children. In families where this is the case, a fracture of the parent-teen relationship can easily occur. In single-parent and step-families, much care needs to be taken to ensure that boundaries are not violated. Children need to remain children and not be burdened with taking care of the emotional well-being of a mom or dad without a partner.

During the teen years, your child revisits this earlier developmental period but with the raging hormones of bursting sexuality (rather than the sensuality of the four- to six-year-old). The dilemma for the parent-child relationship is even more salient as mom or dad is confronted with a blossoming young lady or man who looks like the spouse that he or she fell in love with some years earlier—but possibly even more beautiful or handsome! If the parents are not comfortable with their own sexuality and warmly erotic with each other, this sudden attraction to their teenager may cause "incest panic." Particularly in the case of father-daughter relationships, the father is drawn to his offspring in such ways that the possibility of acting feelings out seems real and threatening. Out of this fear he may, consciously or unconsciously, suddenly cut off physical warmth, becoming distant and cold. In this typical scenario, the daughter feels not only abandoned but also rejected because of her new and fragile sexuality and delicate sense of self.

Sadly, so often adolescent girls "lose" their father's affection just when they need it most.

So how can these awkward but common sexual feelings be handled? If we neither wish to withdraw affection nor repress "unthinkable" feelings, what are the options? Held in, these powerful energies can easily build like pressure in a volcano—felt covertly as tension within the family dynamics. This dysfunctional undercurrent can lead to addictions and health problems, including eating disorders. Acted out in sexual ways, these conflicts become perverted, leading to frigidity, impotence and promiscuity. One solution instead of denial is to acknowledge that those feelings exist and are normal.

By coupling compassion with honesty, rather than indulging in denial and repression, you can regulate these forces. First of all, when these sexual sensations arise, notice them for what they are and try to accept them in a non-shaming, non-judgmental way as part of a shared (probably universal) human experience. Next, allow these sensations to move through as waves of pure energy. This vital energy can then be used in creative projects or to re-establish or enhance the erotic connection with your spouse or partner. Handled consciously, conflicts like these can be moved through in this transformative way in a surprisingly short time. Using the somatic (felt-sense) experiencing you learned earlier in this book, allow your sensations to move freely throughout your body as life force energy. If you still find yourself struggling with sexual issues, get professional help to strengthen your own boundaries so that you can model healthy limits, thereby transmitting healthy sexuality to the next generation.

It is very important to speak to your children candidly about sex and to help them form strong boundaries before they reach puberty. This will help them to be less vulnerable to group pressures, date-rape and other assaults. Because reducing the risk of sexual violation (along with early detection of problems) is so important, this topic is covered in more depth in Chapter VI.

Sexual Violation:
Reducing the Risk and Early Detection

Unless you have personally experienced the deep wound of sexual trauma, it may be difficult to imagine how complex, confusing and varied the long-term effects can be. This is especially true when the molestation was perpetrated by someone the child trusted or even loved. When a child's innocence is stolen, it affects self-worth, personality development, socialization and achievement. Violation at a young age plays havoc with later intimacy in adolescent and adult relationships. In addition, these children are prone to somatic symptoms, rigidity, awkwardness or excessive weight gain/loss, born of a conscious or unconscious attempt to find safety by "locking out" others. Because it is painful to be fully present in their body, these children tend to live in a fantasy world and to have problems with attention, spacing out, daydreaming and (what psychologists call) dissociation. These are coping mechanisms that keep their awful experience compartmentalized. This is how violated kids survive; but, of course, they do not thrive unless their hidden wounds are discovered and healed.

This chapter focuses on awareness, prevention and how to approach children in a way that will earn their trust in your ability to protect them so they will tell you what you need to know. It is a guide to help you recognize what sexual trauma is, assist you in safeguarding your children without frightening them, illustrate ways to help them develop healthy boundaries and support you in creating an atmosphere of healthy sexuality within your current family. It is far less likely that children will be victimized if they have parents who listen for opportunities to discuss topics of touch and sex. In addition, they need parents who foster body awareness and can be counted on to believe and defend them.

Sexual Trauma Symptoms

The sexual molestation and assault of children has the added shroud of secrecy and shame. In addition, less than ten percent of predation is perpetrated by a stranger. Because children are usually violated by someone they know and trust, the symptoms are layered with the complexity of the repercussions of betrayal. Children are often asked to keep the activity secret—or worse, threatened with physical harm if they tell.

Fear-stricken children often do not tell us with words. If their assailant is an authority figure, such as a parent, coach, teacher or clergy, children blame themselves. They carry the shame that rightly belongs to the molester. Frequently they hide their pain because they fear punishment, revenge or the refusal of others to believe them. Sadly, this is all too often the case. Though their lips may be sealed, children show us many signs that they have been violated. Be suspicious if you see any of the symptoms from the following list:

1. Sexualized behavior that is not age-appropriate. Some examples are: masturbating in public, simulating intercourse, using seductive or sensual gestures with an adult, French kissing or touching an adult's genitals.

2. Sudden refusal, reluctance or fear at being left alone with a certain person or in a particular place that the child once enjoyed.

3. Withdrawal from other children or difficulty making friends. (Violated children tend to be the loners on the playground, clinging to a safe adult such as a teacher, aide or counselor.)

4. Pain, burning, itching or bruising in the genital and/or anal areas.

5. An unusual discharge that may be indicative of a sexually transmitted disease.

6. An indirect revelation on the part of the child. Examples are: "I don't want to be an altar boy anymore." "Jill's daddy wears underpants with teddy bears on it." "What does it mean when a man puts his penis in somebody's mouth?"

7. General symptoms such as bedwetting, returning to earlier behaviors like thumb-sucking, difficulty sleeping and eating. Inability to concentrate, dreaminess, living in a fantasy world and other variations of dissociation are especially common.

8. Personality changes such as chronic irritability, sudden mood shifts, excessive shyness and postures that reveal a sense of shame, guilt or secrecy.

Note: Physical or sexual abuse almost always requires the additional support of a professional trauma therapist. But whether a particular child needs a therapist or not, there is a lot that you as parents can do to prevent and heal trauma.

Children do not tell that they have been molested unless they are asked in a way that makes them feel safe to tell. Parents need to set the groundwork to earn their child's trust. They need to make the following clearly understood:

1. That children have a right to their own body and who is allowed to see it or touch it.

2. That they will be believed rather than blamed, punished or shunned if they tell you that they have been approached.

3. That their feelings will be understood (not overlooked) and that they will be sheltered from further harm.

4. They also need to know that it is *never ever* their fault.

Reducing the Risk of Sexual Wounds

Sexual trauma varies widely from overt sexual assault to covert desires that frighten and confuse a child by invading his or her delicate boundaries with un-bounded adult sexual energies. When parents have had unresolved sexual violations themselves or were lacking models for healthy adult sexuality, it may be difficult to protect children without conveying a sense of fear and rigidity around issues of touch, affection, boundaries and sensuality. Parents might even avoid offering either discussion or protection due to their own lack of experience in sensing, within themselves, the difference between safe or potentially dangerous situations and people.

No child, even with solid parental support, is immune to the risk of molestation. In fact, conservative reports from as far back as the 1950s estimate that one out of every four individuals worldwide has suffered sexual violations—many of these as children under the age of thirteen. With females, the risk is even higher.[1] Imagine this statistic next time you are shopping in the supermarket. Clearly if you or your child has been abused, you are not alone! If your child suffers from sexual trauma, by all means seek the help of a therapist. It is best to find a professional who is experienced in working with sexually traumatized children.

Are Some Children More Vulnerable Than Others?

The majority of parents, communities and school programs warn children to avoid "dangerous strangers." Sadly, strangers are seldom the problem. Other myths persist, such as the one that only girls are vulnerable, and that most assaults happen at or after puberty. Although statistics vary, the numbers of preschoolers and school-age children reporting sexual assault are astonishing.

Approximately 10% of sexual violations happen to children less than five years old[2]; more children between eight and twelve report molestation than teenagers; and 30 to 46% of all children are sexually violated in some way before they reach the age of eighteen.[3] *Sexual trauma is pervasive—it prevails no matter the culture, socio-economic status or religion.* It is not uncommon within the "perfect" family. In other words, all children are vulnerable; and most sex offenders are "nice" people that you already know! If you have been putting off talking with your children about sexual molestation until they are older or because you are uncomfortable with the topic, we hope that what you learn here will bolster your confidence to begin these discussions sooner rather than later.

The Twin Dilemma of Secrecy and Shame

The sexual molestation of children has the added shroud of secrecy. Since *85 to 90% of sexual violations and inappropriate "boundary crossings" are by someone the victims know and trust,* the symptoms are layered with the complexity of betrayal.[4] Even if not admonished (or threatened) to keep the assault secret, children often do not tell due to embarrassment, shame and guilt. In their naiveté they mistakenly assume that they are "bad." They carry the shame that belongs to the molester. In addition, children fear punishment and reprisal. They frequently anguish over "betraying" someone who is part of their family (or social circle) and worry about what might happen to their perpetrator. This fear is especially strong if it is a family member they are dependent on or love.

If not a family member, the violator is usually someone well known. Neighbors, older children, babysitters, a parent's boyfriend, other members of the family or step-family, as well as "friends" of the family, are frequently the offenders. Or it may be someone who has prestige and social status or serves as a mentor, such as a religious leader, teacher or athletic coach. For example, the BBC News reported in February 2004 that 11,000 cases went on record of American youths sexually abused by more than 4,000 priests. Since that time *many* more cases have been discovered. How can children know—unless you teach them—that they are not to blame when the perpetrator is usually not only someone known, but someone who may be revered? Parents can pave the way to safety for their children by teaching them to trust and act on their own instincts versus submitting to an older child or adult who is using their power for their personal sexual gratification.

What Is Sexual Violation?

If sexual violation isn't typically a "dirty old man" luring a child with candy into his car, what is it? Simply put, it is any time that anyone takes advantage of their position of trust, age or status to lead a child into a situation of real or perceived powerlessness around issues of sex and humiliation. In other words, when children must passively submit to the will of another rather than having the choice to defend themselves or tell someone, whether or not they are "forced," it constitutes sexual violation or assault. This can range from being shown pornography by a teenaged babysitter, to an insensitive medical examination of a child's private parts, to being forced to have sexual intercourse with a parent or other adult. While actual rape by a parent or step-parent is less common, exposure to pornographic material or being asked to strip, look at or handle exposed genitals, as well as rough handling during medical procedures, is far too common.

Steps Caregivers Can Take to Decrease Children's Susceptibility

1. **Model Healthy Boundaries:** No one gets to touch, handle or look at me in a way that feels uncomfortable.

2. **Help Children Develop Good Sensory Awareness:** Teach children to trust the felt sense of "Uh-oh" they may experience as dread in the gut or rapid heartbeat, which lets them know something is wrong and they need to leave and get help.

3. **Teach Children How to Avoid Being Lured:** Teach children how to use their "sense detectors" as an early warning sign.

4. **Offer Opportunities for Children to Practice Saying "No."**

5. **Teach Children What to Say and Do:** Also, let them know that they should always tell you so that you can keep them safe and help them with their feelings.

Let's take a more detailed look at these steps:

1. Model Healthy Boundaries

There is a delightful children's picture book by James Marshall about two hippopotami that are good friends. One's name is George, the other Martha. They visit and play together and have dinner at each other's houses. One day Martha is soaking in her bathtub and is shocked to see George peeking through the window, looking right at her! George was surprised at her outrage, and his feelings got hurt. He thought that this meant Martha didn't like him anymore. Martha reassured George that she was very fond of him. She explained in a kind manner, "Just because we are good friends, George, doesn't mean that I don't need privacy when I'm in the bathroom!" George understood.

This little *George and Martha* story models making boundaries, communicating them clearly and honoring the boundaries of others. Parents need to show good boundaries themselves and to respect children's need for privacy (especially beginning between the ages of five and seven). They need to support their children when they are in situations that are unappealing and are defenseless to keep themselves safe. This begins in infancy. The following illustration will help you understand how to offer this protection:

Little baby Arthur fussed and arched his back each time Auntie Jane tried to hold him. His mother, not wanting to offend her sister, said, "Now, now, Arthur, it's OK, this is your Auntie Jane. She's not going to hurt you!"

Ask yourself what message this gives to Arthur? He is already learning that his feelings aren't important and that adult needs take precedence over a dependent's needs. Babies show us their feelings by vocal protests and body language. They are exquisitely attuned to the vocalizations and facial expressions of their parents. The brain circuits are being formed by these very interactions that are specifically about respect for feelings and boundaries around touch. For whatever reasons, Arthur did not feel safe or comfortable in Aunt Jane's arms. Had his "right of refusal" been respected, he would have learned that his feelings do make a difference, that he does have choices and that there are adults (in this case his mother) who will protect him from other adults whose touch he does not want.

A few tactful words to Jane, such as "Maybe later, Jane—Arthur's not ready for you to hold him yet," would leave a positive imprint on the baby's newly developing sense of self. And if his mother's appropriate protection continues, Arthur's brain is more likely to forge pathways that promote self-protective responses. These may safeguard him from an intrusion and assault later in his life. Although not in his conscious awareness, the unconscious body boundaries formed in these tender years will serve him well into adolescence and beyond.

Trauma is a breach of our boundaries. Sexual trauma, however, is a sacred wound—an intrusion into our deepest, most delicate and private parts. Children, therefore, need to be protected by honoring their right to personal space, privacy and to be in charge of their own body. As different situations develop at various ages and stages, children need to know that they do not have to subject themselves to "sloppy kisses," lap-sitting and other forms of unwanted attention to please the adults in their lives.

**Other Areas Where Children Need Respect and Protection
of Boundaries**

Children instinctively imitate their parents. Adults can capitalize
on this favorable attribute when it comes to toileting behavior. A
lot of power struggles and unpleasantness for toddlers and parents alike can be avoided altogether. By respecting your child's
timetable, she will joyfully model mom's behavior and toilet-"train"
herself. Take the "train" out of toileting and your little boy will
proudly do it "like daddy does" at his own pace. Prevent unnecessary trauma in this major developmental stage by following your
child's lead rather than listening to the "experts" who believe in
timetables.

The Learning Channel showed a documentary of a family dealing with the trials of having had multiple-births. The mother was
struggling with toilet-training several of the younger children (as
well as with the needs of her three older children). She turned this
often grueling task that can be filled with shame and embarrassment into an exciting "rite of passage." First, she gave each of these
young children their own training toilet, reinforcing a sense of personal space. She then created a "Poop Book" for the children, which
the entire family helped decorate, that would chronicle when and
who had made a potty. This created a sense of excitement and support in the family. The older children learned to look for signs when
the younger ones needed to go and not only alerted their mother,
but cheered, helped and sometimes even carried their young siblings to the bathroom! Once one had done it, all the rest were eager
to follow suit.

We are not saying that you can't expedite toilet-training, but
forcing a child who is not ready to use the toilet disrespects his
right to control his own bodily functions and sets a life-long pattern that being dominated by someone else is to be expected. By
encouraging rather than pushing, you will be assisting your

children to develop healthy self-regulatory habits and a natural curiosity about their own body. In some cases, you may even be preventing eating disorders, digestive problems, constipation and related difficulties—and as a side effect, produce happy, joyful and spontaneous children.

2. Help Children Develop Good Sensory Awareness

You already have a good start on step number two if your family has been practicing awareness of sensations. Earlier in this book you learned how to locate and name bodily sensations, then focus attention on them long enough to experience a change. Protecting children from sexual abuse begins by talking about different kinds of touch, checking in with various sensations that touch can provoke and teaching kids to trust their instincts when the touch feels uncomfortable, unsafe, frightening, painful, or makes them feel "dirty," secretive or ill-at-ease. All of these, of course, are physical sensations.

A pilot project used in schools called "Child Sexual Abuse Prevention Project, Minneapolis, Minnesota" explains touch in a simple manner on a continuum from "good touch" to "confusing touch" to "bad touch." It describes good touch as feeling like something has been given. Children, when asked what types of touch feel good, will usually mention a hug, petting an animal, playing games, a soft blanket wrapped around them, cuddling, back rubs with mommy and daddy, etc. Examples of bad touch include hitting, pushing, hair-pulling, spanking, aggressive tickling and touching genitals or breasts—in short, any touch that is not wanted.

In addition to touch that clearly feels "good" or "bad," there is a touch that may confuse a child. Something about it just doesn't feel right. It may frighten or overwhelm them, but they tolerate it because it comes from an older person they love or respect. Or it may be confusing because it feels pleasurable to receive the special attention and "private time," but fear surrounds the secrecy. Sometimes the touch itself may feel both pleasurable and sickening at the same time, compounding the confusion.

Teaching children to be savvy by trusting their felt sense, intuition and confused feelings as a red-alert to danger can go a long way in preventing sexual abuse. Before they fall into a dangerous situation, they may feel a sensation of dread in the pit of their stomach or a rapid heartbeat and sweaty palms that let them know something is very wrong with what they are seeing, hearing or being asked to do. It is a signal to get help from someone they trust. Sometimes children's guts register a vague "Uh-oh" type of early warning signal. Or children may feel a sense of shame, embarrassment or guilt without understanding why. They may experience outright disgust that literally makes them feel sick to their stomach. At other times, they will know something isn't right because they feel numb, helpless, paralyzed or frightened. It is especially important to *practice what to do or say beforehand*—because once a child feels a sort of paralysis, a plan of action would be very difficult to formulate and execute.

In any case, you can train your children to: 1) recognize and trust their inner sensations; 2) ask for help immediately (from you or someone nearby they feel safe with) if they experience any bad, uncomfortable or confusing feelings; 3) be assured that you will believe and protect them no matter who the person is or what that person told them or threatened would happen if the "secret" is revealed.

3. Teach Children How to Avoid Being Lured

In addition to being trained how to trust their "sense detectors" as an early warning sign, children also need to be taught what traps to avoid. Again, if they know in advance that there are a few older children and adults in every neighborhood who have problems and may try to take advantage of them, they are less likely to blame themselves if approached. They are also less likely to "take the bait."

In *No More Secrets* by Caren Adams and Jennifer Fay, the authors suggest that if a request ...

- feels funny
- seems like it would separate her/him from other children
- goes against family rules
- involves a secret
- seems like an unearned "special" favor

... children should refuse the request, report it and expect your support in backing them up no matter who the authority figure is or how convincing he might appear.[5] ▪

Depending on the age of your child, it is important to give direct information. You might define sexual molestation by describing it as: someone touching you, looking at you or asking you to touch them or look at them in a way that gives you a funny, confusing or uncomfortable feeling. But it is also useful to name specific body parts and possible situations rather than to be vague. For example, you might say to a teenage girl, "Someone may brush up against your breasts and pretend it was accidental." To a school-aged child you might say, "An older child, teacher or other grown-up may want to touch your penis (vagina, anus) in the washroom." Give a variety of different examples relevant to your child's age, understanding and situation. To a preschool child, you might explain, "Someone may want to hold you too close, rub against you or put his hands in your pants." Again, the more that you respect your child's boundaries, the better she will be at register-ing and reporting inappropriate touch. Later in this chapter, we have some boundary-strengthening exercises for your family that will reinforce the principles that you are learning here.

Children Need to Know Who the "Someone" Might Be

Children, of course, need to be warned about taking rides, candy, gifts, etc., from strangers. They also need to be told that this potentially dangerous "someone" may be a next-door neighbor, a relative, a babysitter, their teacher, coach, scout leader, recreation director, older sibling or religious leader. They need to know that people can be nice and still have problems that cause them to do mean things sometimes. They also need to know that other children (almost always abused themselves) may be sexual abusers.

In reviewing the research for this chapter, one of the most startling statistics uncovered was the large percentage of children molested by older brothers and teenage babysitters. "The estimates are that incest between siblings may be five times more common than paternal incest."[6] Two other statistics from this source are: the average age a sibling is violated is 8.2 years, and the most frequently reported age when abuse begins is five years old! This is a special age when kids are curious, spontaneous and naturally loving. Dispelling the "dirty old man" myth, both the *Child Adolescent Psychiatry Journal* (1996) and the Criminal Justice Source Statistics (2000) report that the average age of most offenders is fourteen, and these fourteen-year-olds also comprise the largest number of sex offenders in any age group.[7] "Fifty-nine percent of child molesters developed deviant sexual interest during adolescence."[8] Adolescent hormones are raging, and teens are often troubled by their newly emerging sexual impulses and drives. Additionally, young teens do not comprehend the long-term damage that is done to vulnerable children and need the guidance of parents to teach them these things.

Children also need to be taught that someone trying to abuse them may use force, but more often they will use trickery. Again, give concrete examples, such as: a babysitter or older child who knows how much you love cats may say, "I'll let you have one of my kittens (or pet my cat), if you will sit on my lap and watch this video." Or the priest from your parish might offer, "You can be an altar boy, but first let's take off your clothes and try these vestments on to see if you're big enough yet." Children also need to know that they may be warned not to tell. If there are threats to keep secrets, your children need to be told that the person who intimidated them has done something wrong. They must tell you so you can protect them from harm.

4. Offer Opportunities for Children to Practice Saying "No"

In order for children to develop the capacity to stop someone from improper, hurtful, uncomfortable or confusing touch, they must have practice and experience with the right of refusal in other areas of their life. In this way it becomes a natural part of their self-confidence and is imprinted in their developing brain.

This process happens when parents respect children's likes and dislikes and allow them to make age-appropriate choices whenever possible. Examples of this are choices in food, clothing and play activities. Parents show disrespect by forcing a child to wear something she dislikes or eat something distasteful just because "I'm your mother (or dad) and I say so!"—instead of saying, for example, "It is (or isn't) healthy for you." If parents chronically disregard a child's feelings, tastes, opinions and sensibilities by overriding them with their own, it leaves an indelible mark in a child's consciousness, communicating that "father knows best" and that authority should never be questioned. It also teaches kids not to trust their own instincts. Adults foster these impressions by saying things such as "How can you be cold when it's so warm outside?" or "Don't color those flowers blue—they're supposed to be orange!" or "You get to choose when you're a grown-up."

When children grow up in this type of authoritarian climate, they cannot be expected to have their wits about them to suddenly say "no" to an adult (especially one who taught them to put their own feelings aside for the sake of the grown-up) when they are under stress and are confused or frightened. These children, then, are the most vulnerable to blaming themselves and feeling chronically ashamed, guilty and isolated if they are lured into a sexual assault. Children who grow up knowing that their choices are valued and their grown-ups will protect them from intrusive, rough or otherwise unpleasant handling by another are more likely to assert their right to say "No!" when they sense that they are about to be trapped in a dangerous situation.

This boundary-setting behavior begins by parents attending to a baby who is fussing because he has been picked up by someone he doesn't feel safe with. It is important for parents to stop older siblings or classmates from bullying, tickling beyond toleration, punching, biting and kicking. If children do not want to be hugged or cuddled for *whatever* reason, they should not be forced or belittled. If we ignore or ridicule children's right to control touch and make boundaries, how will they be able to protect themselves later in life? Instead we must honor each child's non-verbal "no" and give him lots of practice in saying "No," "Stop" or "Don't." Children have an instinctive sense about who is safe and who is not. You, the parents, need to trust this sense and foster its development rather than try to change a child's mind.

Since the molester is most often a family friend or relative, it is common for the assault to happen in small stages over time. Often it starts with lewd thoughts long before an actual assault takes place. The following story illustrates just how important it is to listen to your children.

JENNY AND UNCLE SHERMAN

When Jenny was eight years old, she began to get a "funny feeling" around her Uncle Sherman but could not understand why. She loved to play with her cousins but was more relaxed when they visited her house. Now, at twelve, she figured out why she was so guarded. Jenny came back from an overnight stay quite upset. The next day, she told her mother that when her uncle played the "wrestle game" with the kids, Sherman pinned her down and intentionally rubbed his body on hers, gently brushing up against her newly developing breasts.

Jenny's mother dismissed this "red flag" and protected her brother's reputation rather than protecting Jenny! She told her daughter that Uncle Sherman "would never do anything like that, was a nice man and probably touched her by accident in play." Her mother missed a clear opportunity to reinforce Jenny's gut feelings and protect her from future attacks by having a frank talk with Uncle Sherman about what happened and how it affected his niece so that he would never treat Jenny or any other child that way again. In addition, she could make sure that he would not be allowed to be alone with Jenny. Sadly, she also missed an opportunity to help her daughter sort out her feelings and to teach her what to do or say if anything similar happened again.

Instead, Jenny had to deal with her feelings alone. She felt uncomfortable with her budding sexuality because of what happened with Uncle Sherman and became ashamed of her body. She also thought, like most children who aren't informed, that something was wrong with her or this would never have happened.

When Jenny was sixteen her mother asked Uncle Sherman to pick his niece up from school and bring her home while her car was being repaired. Jenny was shocked when Uncle Sherman began to drive toward the mountains rather than toward her house. He said he was going to take his favorite niece for a hamburger.

After eating, they continued toward the mountains. When they arrived in an isolated wooded area, he told her how much he had always "loved" her, yearned for her and asked if she would remove her bra so that he could make her feel "really good." Not having a clue what to do, Jenny sat in her uncle's truck motionless while he continued his assault by undoing the clasps himself.

Remember how Jenny distrusted Uncle Sherman as early as age eight! Perhaps she felt those "icky" sensations because of the lewd way he looked at her, or maybe she sensed a strong sexual energy directed at her that made her feel uncomfortable. If Jenny's mother had taught her that even family members sometimes do hurtful things, taken her daughter's instinctual feelings seriously, validated her discomfort and taken action to protect Jenny, the later sexual assault could have been avoided. Jenny most likely wouldn't be struggling with painful feelings now, as an adult, whenever her loving husband desires to admire or touch her breasts.

5. Teach Children What to Say and Do

Just as naturally as you teach children about other safety issues, such as crossing the street, calling 911, wearing seat belts and water safety, you can teach them the difference between "good" touch and "secret" (confusing or bad) touch. Often, however, parents assume that children understand what this is and how to respond when actually they do not! One way to test their comprehension after a "talk" is to ask them to use their own words to tell you what they think you mean. Another way is to role-play possible scenarios, tailoring them to your child's vulnerabilities and age. Children learn best through games and guided practice.

In *No More Secrets*, the authors offer four different games that provide enjoyable rehearsals.[9] These are paraphrased from that book and described below:

Games for Kids to Practice Making Boundaries

What If . . .

This is a good game to play to check understanding and to practice plans for a variety of situations. The whole family asks questions and creates different answers. Sample questions to stimulate children's thinking are:

- What if your bicycle got a flat tire and someone offered to give you a lift home?

- What if a bully took your ball and told you to follow him to his garage to get it?

- What if the new neighbor down the street asks if you can keep a secret?

Storytelling

This is a way to provide positive, concrete examples of children acting on their own behalf and being successful. A story might go like this:

There was a little boy who had an older brother who always bought him whatever he wanted. But the brother would scare him by hiding and jumping out at him in the dark. The little boy didn't like to be scared, but he didn't know what to do. One day he asked his father if he was ever scared. His dad said, "Sometimes." The little boy asked him how he got unafraid. Dad asked him if something was frightening him, so the little boy told about his big brother. His dad helped him figure out that he could tell his brother not to do that anymore and could come to Dad if the brother still didn't stop.

Face-Off or "Space Invaders"

This game helps children understand their own body space and boundary needs. Two children stand face to face, back up from each other about fifteen feet, and then slowly walk toward each other until one of them becomes uncomfortable with the closeness. They can then point to or name the place in their body that feels uncomfortable and describe what the sensation feels like. They can then be encouraged to make a movement and sound or word that lets the other child know they do not have permission to come closer. Have them practice until their body language shows that they really mean it.

Children may goof off at first and bump into each other, but they can tell the point where they are too close as a sign to protect their "space." Have them try the same game side by side and back to back or approach each other from different angles. After children explore body space boundaries with each other, they can practice with an appropriate adult if they wish. The adult might play different roles, first pretending to be a stranger, then an acquaintance and then someone well-known, like a parent or neighbor. The game can help children identify quickly when someone is invading their space. This reinforces refinement of (and trust in) their own body clues and instinctive signals that we talked about earlier.

"No!"

This game increases the likelihood that children will say "No" when they need to.

1. Brainstorm rules that seem to encourage children to do things they might not want to do.

Examples:

- Be nice to people.

- Don't hurt people's feelings.

- Don't be rude. If someone speaks to you, answer.

- You are responsible for taking care of other people.

- Think of others' needs before your own.

- Don't question adult authority.

- Always obey the babysitter.

"Rules" like these—named, discussed and acknowledged—lose power and everybody can make choices about when it might be good to follow those rules and when it's better to say "No!"

2. Practice saying "No!"

Start by having two children or one child and one adult take turns asking pretend favors. Start with a simple "No!" answer that the partner must accept. Adapt the difficulty level as children become more skilled by saying things like: "What's the matter, don't you like me anymore?" and then see where it leads. Be sure to give the children chances to say "No!" to adults.

You may be surprised at how easily children "cave in" to adult requests. They think they are being mean, disobedient or disrespectful to do otherwise. This game can help you assess how your children might behave in a potential assault situation and give you a chance to help them practice being confident and strong in saying "No!"

Help your child to counter learned physical helplessness around people who are bigger, stronger or have authority over him. In addition to the games above, organized sports, martial arts, fitness exercises, running games, arm wrestling and other activities like a special kids' "model mugging" class can promote a sense of physical competence as an antidote to a sense of helplessness.

Why Most Children Don't Tell: Making It Safe for Them to Tell You

In *Miss America By Day,* Marilyn Van Derbur poses the question: "Is it safe for children to tell?" She answers that rhetorical question: "Only if you and I make it safe."[10] What does she mean by this? She goes on to cite research that the average age of first-time violation is five to six years old. Those who told a parent before age eighteen encountered the following negative parental reactions (some experienced multiple responses):

- Anger with them (the child) (42%)

- Blamed them (49%)

- Ignored the disclosure (50%)

- Became hysterical (30%)

Although it may seem unbelievable, the average child never tells! As a school psychologist, I can attest to this by the fact that countless children told me that I was the first one they ever confided their secret to! Children typically fear blame and punishment. Common responses I have heard are "She would kill me if she knew!" "My mother/father would just call me a liar." "She wouldn't do anything anyway because she wouldn't want to upset him." "He'll say it was entirely my fault."

The good news is that you can cultivate a climate of safety in your household. And it will pay big dividends for your youngsters. Another study attests to the benefits: "Those who told immediately or very shortly after the abuse and were believed and supported showed relatively few long-term traumatic symptoms. Those who either did not tell (typically due to fear or shame) or who told and then encountered a negative, blaming, disbelieving or ridiculing response were classified as extremely traumatized."[11] Ms. Van Derbur wrote that when she first started advocating on behalf of children, she had bumper stickers made and placed on hundreds of cars that read "BELIEVE THE CHILDREN."

To increase the odds that your child will tell you: 1) Teach them about inappropriate touching as early as preschool; 2) Let them know it is never their fault; 3) Teach and role-play when and how to tell you or another safe adult; 4) Let them know in advance that you will believe and protect them; 5) Let them know that you will never reject or punish them. In other words, make it easy for your child to tell!

Date Rape and Other Teen Issues

Teens who have had early unresolved sexual wounds or who have grown up without healthy role models in the areas of personal privacy, boundaries and sexuality may find it difficult to even be aware of personal safety, let alone practice it, on-the-spot when they begin dating.

If their feelings, opinions and rights were disregarded or minimized by parents, grandparents or older siblings, these teens—who may never have practiced saying "no" at home (and have it respected)—are headed for trouble when they find themselves on a date, alone with a boy, in a car on a dark night or even on a high school campus in broad daylight!

Unfortunately, date rape in high school and college happens far too often. One landmark study in the U.S. reported that one in four college women was the victim of rape or attempted rape.[12] Parents need to establish ongoing conversations with pre-teens and teens. Find out what your son's and daughter's concepts are regarding acceptable and unacceptable behavior under various circumstances. Don't assume that adolescents can make clear judgments when their hormones are raging, or that they don't need your guidance because they suddenly are in adult bodies. Teens often need more guidance at this important juncture of their lives than at any other time.

Echoes into the Next Generation: Transforming the Legacy

It doesn't help matters that we live in a culture where there is so much confusion around sexual values and behaviors. Often overlooked is the fact that sexual energy and life force energy are virtually one and the same. People who have passion for life have a flow of creative energy that feels inspiring and uplifting to be around. It is life-positive. They are considered to be "juicy"; those around them soak up their spark and creative exuberance. Instead of being the norm they stand out.

What is creative life force anyway? Where does it originate? In Indian culture, it is referred to as "second-chakra energy" and it arises from our sexual organs. It is the arousal energy that made troubadours sing and the great masters compose, build, paint, create theater and write literature that delights us and endures through time. It is the energy of both creation and procreation. So much fear exists about this potent force that social and religious institutions have traditionally tried to dampen it down.

Unfortunately, when a lid is put on feelings and sensations that are normal—making ordinary folks confused and guilt-ridden—it is difficult for flesh-and-blood human beings to know what to do when these strong feelings arise unbeckoned. Attempts to dictate what thoughts, feelings and sensations are proper or improper is a breeding ground for shame. Thoughts are thoughts and sensations are sensations. Period! They do not need to be acted out inappropriately.

When the moral judgment is removed, individuals are able to acknowledge and experience their authentic life energy freely. Without having to deny or repress them, healthy decisions and expressions of sexuality are more likely. The unspeakable becomes spoken and families can become a model for shaping healthy behavior.

On one more note, we wish to acknowledge the reality that many successful families may be "non-traditional"—having two parents of the same sex, being a single-parent, step-family or blended family—yet we trust that some of the ideas presented here will have relevance to your particular situation.

All families need nurturing touch such as hugging, holding, cuddling and massage. It is never acceptable, however, for an adult or older child to satisfy their own needs for comfort, nurturance, power or sexual gratification by exploiting a child (or anyone) who is incapable of understanding and protecting themselves against a choice they were not free, or did not perceive they were free, to make.

This chapter is by no means exhaustive. There are many wonderful books to help parents talk to their children about healthy sex, normal sexual development and sexual assault. *No More Secrets* by Caren Adams and Jennifer Fay, which is quoted here, may be an "oldie" but it is a gem of a "goodie." Also, *Miss America By Day* by Marilyn Van Derbur gives a meticulous, personal and far-reaching account of the long-term effects of sexual abuse. It is an invaluable guide to the prevention of sexual violation of children. The CD *Sexual Healing, Transforming the Sacred Wound,* by Peter A. Levine (Sounds True, 2003) is an audio learning series that includes various guided exercises; it is a useful companion to this chapter for teens and adults.

——

CHAPTER VII

Separation, Divorce and Death: Helping Your Child Move through the Grieving Process

The focus of this chapter is on helping your child cope with the grief that accompanies separation and loss. Sometimes the leave-taking is temporary, such as when a parent travels frequently for work or is in the military. Sometimes the loss is unexpected, abrupt and permanent like a tragic accidental death or terminal illness. Perhaps the threat of a separation has been looming like a dark cloud for a long time, as often happens in divorce. In any case, kids are affected to varying degrees and can suffer from both stress and deep sorrow. When the parting is like a bolt from the blue, shock and grief are inextricably woven together. The following information is offered to assist you in guiding your child through the painful terrain of both.

Symptoms of Grief versus Symptoms of Trauma

Whenever there is trauma, there is grief. Grief is the emotion that accompanies loss. Whether the trauma is from a disaster, such as a fire or flood, or from a betrayal, such as molestation or abandonment, something of great value has been lost. Whether the loss is material, such as a home and personal possessions, or something as intangible as the loss of innocence, the sense of the world as a safe place is gone. It is possible to have grief without trauma; it is not possible to have trauma without grief.

The symptoms of grief and trauma are different. When a child experiences deep sadness—such as with the death of an old, ill pet—it is easier, and often helpful, to talk about it. With shock-trauma, a child is left speechless. If a puppy is struck by a car right in front of a child's eyes, the grief becomes complicated by trauma. Because the death was unexpected and dramatic, the feelings and images cannot be assimilated all at once. The horror needs to be worked through so that the shock of it can be released from the child's body and psyche.

In contrast to the day-to-day reality of caring for an ailing pet through its final days, the tragic death of an active dog or cat seems unreal. While grief feels emotional and real, shock seems surreal. This is one major difference between trauma and grief, despite the fact that in both cases, the loss of a pet is a painful experience.

In 2001 social researchers William Steele and Melvyn Raider compiled a chart illustrating significant ways in which trauma reactions differ from grief reactions.[1] Our adapted comparison below is more suited to our body-based approach.

GRIEF	TRAUMA
Generalized reaction is SADNESS	Generalized reaction is TERROR
Grief reactions stand alone	Trauma generally includes grief reactions
Grief reactions are known to most professionals and some laypeople	Trauma reactions, especially in children, are unknown to the public and many professionals
In grief, talking can be a relief	In trauma, talking can be difficult or impossible
In grief, pain is the acknowledgment of loss	In trauma, pain triggers terror, a sense of loss, of overwhelming helplessness, and loss of safety

GRIEF *(continued)*	**TRAUMA** *(continued)*
In grief, anger is generally non-violent	In trauma, anger often becomes violent to others or self (substance, spousal & child abuse)
In grief, guilt says, "I wish I would/would not have ..."	Trauma guilt says, "It was my fault. I could have prevented it" and/or "It should have been me instead"
Grief generally does not attack nor "disfigure"our self-image and confidence	Trauma generally attacks, distorts, and "disfigures" our self-image and confidence
In grief, dreams tend to be of the deceased	In trauma, dreams are about self as potential victim with nightmarish images
Grief generally does not involve trauma	Trauma involves grief reactions in addition to specific reactions like flashbacks, startle, hypervigilance, numbing, etc.
Grief is healed through emotional release	Trauma is released through discharge and self-regulation
Grief reactions diminish naturally over time	Trauma symptoms may worsen over time and develop into PTSD and/or health problems

Why the Distinction between Trauma and Grief Is Important

The distinction between trauma and grief is important for several reasons. While the sadness and sullenness of a bereft youngster is

easy to recognize, often a child who has been stunned by separation suffers silently. She may display behavior problems, headaches
or stomachaches that parents do not link to the stress that she is
going through. Because of this she may be ignored or punished
for her "misbehavior" or misdiagnosed with an elusive medical
problem. When astute parents are savvy enough to make this distinction, children are less likely to suffer from misunderstanding
and mistreatment.

Another reason it is essential to know the difference between
grief and trauma is that the tools to help your child work through
his initial shock reactions are different from the tools that enable
you to guide your child through the grieving process. When a child
is assisted to come out of a shut-down, traumatized state, the mixed
emotions of the grieving process can more freely move through
their normal course. On the other hand, a prolonged state of shock
leaves your child with a lingering sense of powerlessness that
heightens her vulnerability to chronic stress, abrupt mood swings
and later, personality disorders.

When trauma is resolved, children can get on with the business
of both grieving *and* living. When it is not, they may easily get stuck
in a fantasy of how it was then—before the "terrible thing" happened—rather than be in the reality of now. The result is a failure
to develop emotionally. There remains a disruption of a child's life,
as if frozen in time. As remarkable as it may seem, we have witnessed teenagers of divorce draw family portraits of their biological parents still living "happily ever after"; while their step-parents
and step-siblings are conspicuously missing—even a decade later!

Unfortunately, the above example of denial and lack of acceptance of the loss is more the rule than the exception. The grieving
process gets thwarted by a child's traumatic reaction to the divorce,
death or separation. Although the pain of loss cannot be avoided,
it can be felt, expressed and "moved through" as it is put into the
bigger picture of your child's life experiences—those both disap-
pointing and rewarding. Helping children untangle shock from

grief and navigate the turbulent waters of divorce and death is the main thrust of this chapter.

Two Views of Divorce: Rosy or Dark?

> I did it for you, and the boys,
> because love should teach you joy,
> and not the imitation that your
> momma and daddy tried to show you.
> I did it for you, and for me,
> and because I still believe there's only
> one thing you can never give up,
> or ever compromise on . . .
> and that's the real thing you need in love.
> – *Kenny Loggins ("The Real Thing"*
> *from his album* Leap of Faith*)*

Tammy Wynette, a famous American country-western singer, croons about divorce, calling it "a dirty little word"; while pop singer Kenny Loggins writes a poignant song for his daughter Amanda called "The Real Thing," hopeful that she will forgive him for leaving her mother. He sings that he doesn't want her to mistake what she sees for "the real thing," fearful that Amanda will confuse the stressful marital dynamics for love.

We all know that there is no escaping the painful journey that begins when a family is in the process of breaking apart. Experts have published conflicting research on the long-term effects of divorce on adult children in terms of happiness and success in marriage, career and life in general. Currently, two extreme views exist: 1) Parents *should* stay together "for the sake of the children" because divorce leaves permanent scars that will follow them into their adult relationships; and 2) Parents *shouldn't* stay together for the children because, as Kenny Loggins sings, an unhappy marriage is a poor model for relationships, and the kids will be adversely affected by the sham. Worse still, it is presumed that they will repeat the pattern when they get married, being almost hypnotically attracted to what feels, sounds and looks "familiar."

An article entitled "Two Portraits of Children of Divorce: Rosy and Dark" by Mary Duenwald (*The New York Times,* March 26, 2002) examined the findings in both camps regarding the adult prognosis for children of divorce, with interesting theories on both sides. According to research by Dr. Judith Wallerstein, children of divorce typically end up ill-prepared to form their own intimate relationships. It's not that they don't recover, but they certainly do need help.[2] On the more optimistic side, Dr. Mavis Hetherington's studies—published in her co-authored book, *For Better or Worse: Divorce Reconsidered*—showed that although divorce is always traumatic for children, resulting in deep sorrow and pain, by the third year there is generally a fairly good adjustment.[3] It is also important to note that although 20 to 25% of children from divorced families show psychological and academic difficulties, so too do 10% of children from families where the parents have remained married. Of course, in cases of domestic violence and child abuse, divorce was always the best choice.

Even more important, Dr. Hetherington found that the single best predictor of children doing well is *the presence of an involved, competent, caring adult* who has high standards for behavior. On the other hand, when children were caught in the middle—in the crossfire between parents—they had the worst possible prognosis for later success. Girls from this group frequently were depressed and anxious; whereas boys in this group were more aggressive and displayed anti-social behavior. When one parent demeans the other parent, sustaining the conflict after the divorce, it causes extreme distress.

Regardless of disparate views, both sides agree unequivocally: divorce hurts! Whether it is hostile or mutual, the child's relationships, living arrangements, financial circumstances and family life are changed forever. Because of both their dependency status and their developmental needs, children are the most vulnerable, and their emotional needs *must* take priority even as parents may be dealing with their own devastating grief (which they need to get help with for themselves). Children experience the family coming apart as "their divorce," asking revealing questions such as "Do we have to get divorced?" The adults suffer, but the children clearly suffer more.

Surviving Divorce: A Guide to Preserving Your Child's Wholeness

Fortunately, we don't believe that parents have to make a choice between two extreme outcomes. Between the "black and white" conclusions from research studies, there are a lot of "gray" areas that encompass factors *within* your control. Although some studies included children who had received grief counseling to support them in making adjustments to a new family structure, none of these reported studies included helping children work through their shock. Typical grief counseling involves talking, listening and helping a child to release their sadness and anger.

Although none of the counseling support mentioned in the research included working with the body, there is no lack of understanding about what the pain of going through a divorce feels like. In her article "Divorce: 10 Things I Learned," freelance author Vicki Lansky wrote the following about her own experience:

> Going through divorce is a physical experience. This one took me by surprise. My *body* seemed to experience a death-defying whirlpool. I hate speed, roller coasters and the feeling of one's stomach dropping when on a turbulent airplane ride. But I can remember having all those feelings ... simultaneously ... while just sitting in a chair after we separated. Yuck! Fortunately this usually passes in three to nine months.[4]

If the above passage is an adult sharing her personal story, can you even begin to imagine what physical experiences children go through who have no control over what their parents do and what happens to them? We believe, however, that when parents divorce in such a way as to focus on becoming *conscious co-parents*, helping their children through the physiological and emotional reactions of shock and grief, the devastating effects of divorce can be significantly reduced. Despite the family's distress, when parents provide the continuity of safety and security to their children by recognizing and honoring their needs, *everyone* fares better in the long run.

Buffering the Shock: What Do You Say and How Do You Talk to Your Child?

Whether you fought in front of the kids, discreetly hid your problems, or "swept them under the carpet" while your marriage died a silent death, divorce pulls the rug out from under a child. Although there is no escaping his reactions, you can certainly buffer some of the shock through preparation. We can't stress enough how important it is for parents to work through their own shock and grief first so as not to burden their kids with their own baggage. This, in itself, will provide a buffer.

Once the parents have had time to assimilate their decision to divorce, they can take the additional time to plan how they will tell the kids and how they will work out the details so that it's as easy as possible for children to make the transition. It's important that your child knows that the parent who is moving out is not divorcing him and will remain an active parent who will still be taking him to soccer practice, tucking him in at night when he sleeps over, etc. Emphasize that the child will have two homes instead of one. It's best that there be sufficient time to help your child get used to the idea little by little. For example, instead of saying, "Your father is having an affair, so I'm kicking him out!" you might say, "Your father and I don't love each other anymore.

But *we both love you* very much. We will be getting divorced from each other, but we will both still be very involved with you."

Asking for your child's input on negotiable decisions, such as how they would like their new room arranged and which parent they want to pick them up from school, can help to empower children at this time when they feel utterly powerless in a circumstance that is entirely beyond their control. Tiny adjustments and creative ideas from your children that you probably wouldn't have dreamed yourself can go a long way toward improving the quality of their lives during an extremely difficult time. In certain decisions, however—such as whose house the child will spend Thanksgiving at—the child may feel burdened with the feelings of the other parent, including loneliness, anger and resentment. Remember to be aware of your children's behavior. If they appear overwhelmed by the decision, help them to talk about how they feel.

Let's take a look at an example of well-meaning parents who didn't take the time to deal with their own reactions to the idea of divorce and did not formulate a plan before telling their son that dad was moving out. After the story, you will learn what they could have said and done instead to help their child with his stunned reactions.

SWEET HEARTBROKEN JACOB

Jacob's parents' marriage had been falling apart for some time. They were both very busy with careers. They spent little time together and seldom argued. They both cherished their son; whenever the couple was together the activities revolved around the three of them. As their professional lives were peaking, their marriage was silently dying. Because they were happy with their individual successes and friendships, no one expected a sudden break-up after fifteen years of a marriage that had been the envy of their friends!

Jacob's father had an affair. His mother detected it immediately. She confronted him. Anger and grief filled the household. Jacob didn't know why. His mother "protected" him, not wanting to say anything bad about his father. Although she went to counseling, she couldn't contain her emotional outbreaks. The affair ended quickly and Jacob's mother forgave her husband, even though he only gave lip service to working on their marriage. He promised to make room for special "couple time" at least once a month.

Jacob was almost thirteen years old and involved in scouting and sleepovers with friends, so this agreement appeared to be a way to rebuild their marriage. This raised hope for Jacob's mom. The couple had one promising weekend before the pattern of living separate lives returned. It took only one couples' counseling session for both of Jacob's parents to realize that their marriage was over.

Reluctantly, Jacob's mother accepted the fact that she had to let go. She also knew how important it was to keep their son's established routines, disrupting his life as little as possible. Both parents agreed that it would be best if Jacob could remain in the same house and school and still have his friends. Since Jacob's dad did not want physical custody, he was to be the one to pack up his belongings and leave. Having arrived at this amicable arrangement in the car on the way home from counseling, his parents never discussed another issue again! They had the illusion that this arrangement was sufficient to protect their son from the impact of divorce.

Without discussing the potential problems or making a plan about how they would tell Jacob, they drove home in an awkward silence. When Jacob was getting ready for bed, they both looked at each other and decided to "get it over with." They went into his room and, without beating around the bush, told Jacob that they were getting divorced and that his dad would be moving out in two weeks.

Jacob went into shock. He didn't cry. He lay on his bed frozen with overwhelm at the sudden news. Both parents, in shock them-selves, held him in their arms. Young Jacob lay silent in bed with his soft brown eyes wide open as if he had just seen a ghost. His skin was pale. His mother tried to console him and let him know that whatever feelings he was having were okay. But Jacob wasn't feeling his emotions. He was numb, paralyzed by the physiologi-cal shock reactions he was having. His parents had no understand-ing or awareness of what he was going through and felt helpless.

Within five to ten minutes after he was told that his dad would be moving out, Jacob said that he had a sharp pain in his chest. He asked his parents to call an ambulance because he was "hav-ing a heart attack." He insisted it had nothing to do with the news of the divorce. He kept repeating, "You don't understand. . . . I'm physically sick. . . . This is a different thing." Unfortunately, they didn't understand that Jacob was in a state of shock. Nor did they understand what shock was or how to deal with it. Had he been able to cry in his parents' arms instead of being overwhelmed by his parents' shocking news, he might have been comforted enough to begin the grieving process.

Discussion: A Happier Scenario for Jacob

Jacob's initial reactions of shock and denial masked his deep grief. He felt misunderstood by his parents—and he was! He went to counseling twice before refusing to continue because he felt mis-understood again—and he was! What Jacob needed was for his parents to help his stuck physical sensations release (as you learned how to do in Chapters II and IV). If he could have been gently guided to release the tightness causing his sharp chest pain, Jacob's sensations might have, in all probability, changed from frozen ter-rified shock into a softening in his chest, allowing his tightly locked tears to flow sooner—as he was held in his parents' arms—rather than much later. *Then* Jacob's emotional responses would have occurred naturally as his body began to open up.

If you refer back to the first five symptoms listed under the "Trauma" column on the "Grief vs. Trauma" chart at the beginning of this chapter, you will notice that Jacob's initial symptoms are all characterized as trauma—not grief! Let's take a closer look:

1. His initial response was terror, rather than sadness.

2. His grief was masked by traumatic shock.

3. Neither parents nor professionals understood his trauma reaction.

4. Jacob did not talk about his feelings—divorce was not a topic he had words for.

5. His pain was a reaction of terror, helplessness and a lost sense of safety rather than of grief.

In other words, Jacob's world had been turned upside down in a few minutes' time. Fortunately, you can do much to avoid the mistakes that Jacob's parents made when and if a divorce or separation is imminent in your own family. Grief is unavoidable, but trauma is preventable! There were two things that could easily have been done for Jacob to soften the blow.

First of all, consider that one of the most predictable high-impact traumatic moments children experience in a family break-up is when the parents first announce that they are getting a divorce. Jacob was stunned by the sudden barrage of devastating announcements. Not only were his parents getting divorced in a decision they made earlier that evening, but in the same sentence he was told that his father would be moving away in two weeks!

While some parents go numb during divorce, others hide their troubled emotions; still others "wear their feelings on their sleeves." None of these states helps a child to cope. What is best for the family is *for the parents to be in touch with their feelings but to contain them* in front of the children so that they can provide solid grounding to help the children digest and process their shock and grief.

Jacob's parents would have been wise to work through their own shock and to process their own emotions *first,* instead of announcing the divorce at bedtime while *they* were still in shock. After having a few days or weeks to recover, his parents could have brainstormed a plan focused on Jacob's needs for stability and continuity. An example might be having Dad find an apartment while continuing to spend some time at home with Jacob for a month or two to get him accustomed to the change. Details of visits with Dad, including how often and how long, would have been worked out in a way that best preserved Jacob's close relationship with his father. Later, Jacob could be involved in making some choices about the arrangement so that he would know he was important, instead of feeling powerless to affect, at least in some ways, circumstances that were forced upon him and for which he bore no responsibility.

Parents can buffer much of the shock at this most vulnerable time by paying very careful attention to how their children are told the bad news. Children need to know the *specifics* of how they will be affected right away. They worry, "Who will take me to swimming lessons or scouts?" "Will I still be able to see my friends?" "Will I be able to get to school on time; who will pick me up?" "Who will Spot, the family dog, go with?"

Simple things like keeping a color-coded calendar for tracking which parent the child will be with on each day and who will transport him to various functions can help your child to feel more secure, knowing that *both* parents will continue caring for him (if this is the case). It also gives your child something to anticipate that's based on reality rather than wishful thinking.

Second, remember that the news, no matter how delicately handled, will still be fraught with some shock reaction. And you already know what to do! Using the same principles learned earlier regarding tracking sensations, images and feelings, you gently guide your child through any frozen, tight or scary feelings and sensations.

Use the steps you learned in Chapters II and IV to assist your child with the shock of accidents, falls and other sudden impacts; the basic principles are essentially the same. The way shock affects the body is similar no matter what the cause.

Earlier, you also learned to assess a shock reaction in your child through quick observation. In the case of Jacob, his pale skin, wide eyes, shallow breath and severely constricted chest muscles (that kept his heart protected from feeling overwhelming grief) were dead giveaways of his trauma. Gently placing a warm, secure and reassuring hand over Jacob's heart—on the spot he said was hurting—until it released might have softened the blow. If you are as fully present as possible, by dealing with your own feelings *first*, you can assist by using this kind of touch in order to bring the needed relief to your child that Jacob, unfortunately, did not receive.

The sensitivity illustrated in the discussion above can easily be applied to each item on the "Eight Most Vulnerable Moments" list below. As you guide your child, it may help you to know that there are predictable times when he or she is most vulnerable to having a traumatic reaction to divorce:

Eight Most Vulnerable Moments for Children When Parents Divorce

1. When you tell your child for the first time that Mom and Dad are getting a divorce

2. When you tell your child that Mom or Dad will move out (or has left)

3. When custody arrangements are being determined

4. When the marriage settlement/financial agreement is being hammered out

5. When your child begins living in a split world: Mom's house/Dad's house

6. When one or both parents start dating

7. When one parent decides to move a long distance away

8. When parents decide to remarry and a step-family is created

Divorce and Children's Development

It is of primary importance when parents separate or divorce that decisions regarding child custody arrangements be based on the developmental and temperamental needs of the child and not based on what's convenient for the parents. Children need close contact with both parents. Recent research shows that this is even truer for infants and toddlers.[5] Security issues are paramount with babies and very young children since they need to feel safe in order to form healthy attachments. Daily visitations are important by the non-custodial parent, if possible. You cannot explain with words to a baby that Dad will be back next week.

Consistency of routines, sensitive transitions and regular visits to the extended family on both sides is usually best. Extended family is especially important if one parent visits infrequently or has abandoned the child. Babies feel safety through their senses. When they are held, rocked, fed, smiled at and otherwise nurtured by the adults in their family circle as often as possible, they will know they are loved by both sides of the family.

As children grow older and begin to separate from their parents, their unique identity is formed through the mirroring given by both mother and father. When they lose contact with one parent, it is as if a part of themselves is bad, has died or both. Be cautious not to diminish the other parent, as it has the predictable effect of diminishing the self-worth of the child as well. Since both parents live inside the child, whether or not you wish that were so, it is the way that it is.

Teenagers usually do fine with less frequent visits, yet they are still in need of strong parental figures who can set firm rules as teens venture forth into the world, becoming more and more independent. Just like toddlers, who want the stability of a parent nearby in case they're needed, teens find that without a firm home base, divorce can be quite disorienting for them as they hazard out into their peer group. Step-parenting can be particularly awkward with teens as they mature physically. Step-daughter and step-father can feel uneasy in the expression of affection. Research data reveal that children ten to fifteen years of age are the least likely to accept a step-parent.[6]

All children need to know that they can remain children even when their family has been permanently restructured. Often what happens, especially in single-parent families, is that children are forced to grow up too soon. If they take on adult responsibilities and emotional burdens, it compromises the development of their own unique identity and sense of self. Luckily, this distortion of self can be prevented by avoiding discord in front of the children (especially when it's about financial or custody issues relevant to them) and not obscuring their childhood needs due to the adult's own pain and inability to cope. If the divorce has been unbearably painful for you, the best way you can help your child is to get professional help for yourself. It can also be helpful for your child to join a "divorce support group" if one is available in your local community or at school.

Almost all children hold two fantasies: one is that their parents will one day reunite, and the other is that they (the children) are, at least in part, to blame for the divorce. This is called "magical thinking," especially common in children between the ages of four and eleven. If they believe they had something to do with the break-up, then they believe they can fix it. This magical thinking must be dispelled. If a parent continues to hold false hopes of remarrying the spouse who has left, it becomes an almost impossible task for the children to accept the divorce and move on.

Another universal belief of children—one that leaves them frightened and shaken—is the fear that since one parent left, the other parent is likely to *leave them,* too. This is especially true of school-age children, who are sure that their behavior had something to do with their mother or father leaving. This age group is also more vulnerable to a variety of fears because they have the capacity for vivid imagination. The best antidote is to make it convenient—yes, even if you despise your ex-spouse—for the children to see him or her as much as possible.

Children often worry, "Who will take care of me?" and "Where do I belong?" If in both mom's house and dad's house kids have a special place of their own that is comfortable, with toys, clothes, books, CDs, stuffed animals or other favorite possessions that stay at each house, it can help a child substantially in knowing they have a firm place in each parent's heart. It's important for them to know that they live at both houses—not live at one and "visit" the other as if a stranger in a strange land. This holds true even though the child may, in fact, spend less time with one parent than the other. And, most of all, reassure, reassure and reassure your son or daughter that parents *don't* divorce children. Adults divorce adults.

Even under optimal circumstances, when a mutual decision is reached by two mature adults who acknowledge that they are no longer a good fit, divorce is not pretty for kids. Knowing that their parents no longer love each other is both painful and inexplicable. It may even leave questions about the foundation of their existence. In addition, explaining to teachers, neighbors and playmates that they live in two places and have two families can be embarrassing and confusing.

It is beyond the scope of this book to discuss the nitty-gritty of differing needs of children during different ages and stages when going through a divorce. The above information summarizes the most critical points for you to be aware of if you plan to, or have already, divorced your partner. There are dozens of excellent divorce books to help adults make decisions that will help kids. The following three are highly recommended: *Mom's House Dad's House,*

Co-Parenting Through Divorce and *Good Parenting Through Your Divorce* (based on the Kid's Turn Workshop Program). There are also many beautiful children's books readily available, such as *Dinosaur's Divorce, The Boys and Girls Book About Divorce, Parents Are Forever* and *It's Not Your Fault, Koko Bear.*

Helping Your Child Grieve

Now that we have addressed how to minimize the traumatic aspects of divorce, we will address your child's grief. There is much you can do to help children cope with painful emotions. When children go through unwanted change and disruption in their lives, they may experience many confusing and conflicting feelings. For example, they may feel anger, hurt and fear while they are also feeling a sense of relief. Other emotions that may be expressed (or repressed) include emptiness, rage, disappointment, loneliness, sadness and guilt.

Learning how to support children through the grieving process is one of the most important ways you can help them to deal with the unsavory twists and turns that are an inevitable part of growing up—and living life in general. Children transform into mature adults not by protection from frustration and pain, but by having skillful parents who, through example, gentleness, compassion and support, help them to face their disappointments and frustration head-on.

Grief is not something that happens only when a person dies. Grief is a sense of loss and sorrow when someone or something we cherished is gone forever. Grief is a part of life. Joy and grief go hand in hand. We can't have one without the other. For children, the most common sources of grief are divorce, death of a grandparent, parent or other relative, the loss of friends who move away, the loss of their home or special possessions and the loss of a pet.

The grieving process is not linear. Nevertheless, the wisdom of the stages of grief that Elizabeth Kübler-Ross delineated many decades ago in her classic book *On Death and Dying* is still a good guide.[7] These stages will be passed through, visited and revisited by your child at various times. Just when you think a child is no longer sad, the feelings pop up again. This can be particularly true on anniversaries, holidays and other circumstances that serve as reminders of her loss.

The *first stage* of grief is *denial* or *disbelief.* A deeper shock reaction frequently occurs at this first stage. If this is the case, you will need to assist your child to move out of this frozen state by helping her identify and feel sensations until they shift and change. This is important so that she does not stay stuck in the fantasy that the death did not happen or that her parents will remarry.

The next two stages deal directly with emotions. In *stage two,* *sadness* and *grief* will emerge. *Stage three* involves feeling *anger* and *resentment.* Stages two and three, in particular, tend to alternate for a while. They also include more nuanced emotions, such as irritability, frustration, emptiness, disappointment and worry. There is nothing more difficult than being separated from someone you love. Being upset is a normal part of the grieving process. When your child is able to express feelings, it is a good sign that he is moving out of the immobility, helplessness and fantasy of the first stage. Your job is to help make a safe "container" to hold your child's heartbreak and anger.

Bargaining is the *fourth stage* of grieving. At this stage it is important to help children maintain a strong sense of self—a sense of confidence that they can handle the pain in the here and now, instead of making a futile attempt to change the circumstances by wishful thinking to bring the past back. This is the stage of pining in which we hear: "If only I had . . . " or "If I woulda', coulda' or shoulda', maybe this 'terrible' thing would never have happened." It may also involve making deals: "If I pray harder or do my chores, please make him come back."

This stage is similar to the first stage—denial. It is denial with a little more thinking, blaming and guilt tossed in. Again, at this stage it is important for your child to receive your help to move through the sensations that accompany her thoughts in order to avoid getting mired down in shame and guilt. Your child can be encouraged to express genuine remorse for what she wishes she had or hadn't done before the person died or left, and then let it go. Later in this chapter you will learn other ways to help your child experience "emotional completion" as a prelude to saying good-bye to a person, pet, traditional family structure or favorite possession.

The *final stage* of grieving is *acceptance* of the reality of what happened, together with the willingness to go on with life to the fullest extent possible—sometimes with even greater vitality and purpose. This is fundamentally different from an attitude of "just get over it" or "it's time to move on" or "burying feelings." It doesn't mean that your child will never feel sad again. It does mean that the energy formerly bound up in a combination of shock and grief reactions has been freed so that there is a genuine sense of completion. Your child's energy can then be used for growing up as she meets the challenges along the road to maturity.

Dealing with the Death of a Pet

For many children the loss of a beloved pet is actually their first experience of profound grief. It is also an opportunity to learn about unconditional love. As mentioned before, grief is not linear. Although there are various stages, children grieve in their own unique way. Some of their behavior may seem illogical to adults. Most young children who are old enough to talk and express feelings will need only that you follow their lead, give compassionate support according to their cues and do your best to give them the space and time they require.

The following story about a little girl's grieving process after the loss of her pet is a shortened version of a letter written to her by her parents to document their respect for their daughter Rachel's grieving process. It shows how Rachel dealt with the stages of grief and shock and how her parents supported her in this process.

FOR RACHEL

On November 15, 2003, your cat, Briar Rose, was killed by neighbor dogs. How you handled this experience at six years old was quite amazing. I jotted it down for you to read when you are older.

When your dad came home from a soccer game, he kneeled down and said he had bad news. "Briar is dead." You wailed for a long time in his arms. Ryan [Rachel's brother] and I were right beside you. You suddenly stopped crying and asked if Rob [Rachel's dad] had Briar. He said he would bring her inside. We all sat by the front door. You held Briar in your lap. She was still warm. As you stroked her, you said many things about her—what a great kitty she was, how she was too young to die and how much you loved her. You also had questions about how she died. Her tongue was hanging out; her eyes wouldn't close. Why not? Are you sure she isn't just asleep? There was no obvious wound, but a bit of blood by her nose. What happened to her? We answered your questions as best we knew, but most importantly, we all supported you, and each other, in letting the sadness out. Rob had wiped away blood from her mouth. All of us were tearful. Then suddenly you said that you were finished holding her and that Rob could take her back outside till we could bury her in the morning.

You were not hungry for dinner, but you sat with us. During our meal you said your head was really hot and you wanted to cool it with water. I suggested a bath ... "no" ... a shower ... "no." You replied instead, "I want to fill up the kitchen sink with cool water and put my head in." You pulled up a chair to the sink, filled it, took off your shirt and dunked your head. You lifted your head from the water and wanted me to time you holding your breath under water—which I did. You had some fun doing that. Then you wanted to call some of your friends. So you phoned friends and left two messages: "Hi, this is Rachel. I'm calling to tell you I am heartbroken because my cat died tonight."

Next, you said you needed to do something to make you laugh. You explained by saying, "When Daddy told me Briar had died, I had just been playing. All that sadness came into me and pushed all my laughter into my feet and now they don't feel good, so I have to do something that will make me laugh."

Moments later, you said everyone was going into the hot tub. When I got in, you said, "Mommy, the laughter got out of my feet!" I asked how, and you said, "Ryan tickled my feet!" I asked where the sadness was now and you said, "All that's left now is love." In the hot tub, you alternately wanted to be held or played with in the water, splashing, sinking and floating.

At bedtime, our usual routine of singing, hand massage and snuggling just seemed to make you sad about Briar. "Mommy, I can't talk about it anymore." So, you put on your headphones and within minutes were asleep.

In the morning, you told me about a dream you had. "I dreamed that there were two Briars—a good Briar and a bad one. The bad cat wanted to eat us up, but the good Briar said she would help us. I held her paw and you, Daddy and Ryan held her other paw and each other's hands and Briar flew us up into the sky with her wings. It was really Briar. Her body came back to me and she saved us."

Later in the morning, you participated in every aspect of Briar's burial. You picked the spot and helped dig the soil. When Rob brought Briar's body out, you were very surprised to notice that she was cold and stiff. We talked about the fact that her spirit and life force weren't in her body anymore. You picked out several crystals that Granddaddy Pete had given to you before he died. You put them in the pillowcase with Briar and said that she wouldn't be alone, that Granddaddy Pete would show her spirit around in heaven.

When the hole was ready, you helped Rob lower her body and put the first dirt on her. We all shared something about her; we were all crying. You knelt down and prayed just like in the pictures of little children—hands folded, head bowed. You weren't quite sure what to say. You helped Ryan shovel, filling the hole with dirt. Then you wanted to sing "Home, Home on the Range," which we did. In the afternoon, you made a cross to put on her grave and wrote "Briar Rose, Rachel's cat, I love you so" adding lots of hearts.

Since then you have had many moments of tears and sadness over Briar. When you see a cat or are reminded of her, you feel your sadness again. It also triggers your sadness "for all my ancestors that I never got to meet." You seem to bring up death more as you hear about it: Jesus dying on the cross, children dying from the flu, etc. We just listen to what you have to say and hold you if you want that.

It is a long process to come to grips with death, but you are doing such a marvelous job. What impressed us so much on that first day was how you knew exactly what you needed to do to help yourself—crazy things like dunking your head and having your feet tickled. We just supported you in your process and you took care of yourself in a most exquisite way. We love you so much, Rachel!

One Year Later

A follow-up with Rachel's mom a few months after Briar's death indicated that Rachel still missed her cat but seemed to be moving through her grief nicely. As the one-year anniversary of Briar's death approached, I checked with Rachel to see how she was doing. Without my mentioning the anniversary, this seven-year-old told me that she still missed Briar and that it was "getting harder" because it was close to the date she died. At her request, Rachel adopted a new cat named Misty. But Misty was not like Briar.

Replacing the loss of Briar, of course, did not do the trick to complete the grieving process. No two pets or people are alike. Children usually adjust to a new pet, friend, step-parent, etc., more easily when they have *completed the five stages* of the grieving process, coming to an acceptance of their loss. That is because prematurely "replacing" a lost animal or person with which a child has formed a deep bond is usually nothing more than a vain attempt to reduce the pain.

It seemed to me that clever Rachel had done much to resolve her grief. She had even "pendulated" between pain and pleasure by alternating between crying and playing. However, she was still hurting. Wondering what might be causing this, I recalled that an obvious piece was missing from her grief process: Rachel never mentioned any regrets or remorse. And there is nothing that brings sorrow, with guilt as its companion, more easily than death. Guilt and regret can occupy a lot of a child's mental and physical energy!

Debunking Common Myths

(The Continuing Story of Rachel and Briar Rose)

Attempting to "replace" the loss of a loved one quickly as a method of resolving grief is a common myth believed by many. Another common myth in our culture is that time alone will heal all wounds. This simply is not so. Of course, time and distance can "take the edge off" the pain; but this is sometimes done at the expense of burying the pain more deeply. This is another myth that adults seem to be adept at believing. Burying the pain is not an efficient method of coping with grief because of several reasons: a) Pain can come back to haunt you unexpectedly; b) Buried pain can create difficulties with bonding and intimacy due to fear of loss or abandonment; c) It takes a "truckload" of energy to keep the buried feelings entombed. In other words, burying pain resolves nothing and teaches people to avoid suffering to their own detriment.

As all spiritual practices and religious philosophies teach, pain is part of life. When children learn to tolerate emotional pain in small doses and realize that if they do, it won't last forever, they have learned one of life's most valuable lessons. They can enter adulthood with solid emotional and physical health, thus feeling more joy and being more resilient human beings.

Time did not heal Rachel's sadness. However, anniversary dates offer another opportunity to complete "unfinished" business because they bring the suppressed emotions quickly to the surface. With the knowledge that Rachel had not "bargained" (stage three), showing remorse for anything she had done or neglected to do prior to Briar's death, I asked her, "Did you take care of Briar?" She explained that she touched her cat, played with her, fed her and gave her water. Next I asked, "Is there anything you wish you had done differently?" Unhesitatingly, Rachel replied, "One thing—I wanted her to feel like she was in a good home." She then went on to explain that she wasn't sure if she had given Briar a good enough home because she held Briar too much when the cat clearly didn't want to be held. Rachel sounded relieved just to let that "cat out of the bag" with her mother and me there to listen as she confessed what she had been holding inside. After Rachel's planned anniversary ceremony for Briar, she will now be able to truly reach the final stage of grieving: acceptance.

More on Resolving Shock and Grief

Another myth about grieving in our modern-day American culture —unlike both old-fashioned extended bereavement rituals and the practices of so-called "primitive" cultures—is that you're supposed to keep your feelings to yourself. In other words, after the funeral is over, if you're not over it, you should grieve alone. In fact, the opposite is true. This is why grief groups are so important in helping both adults and children resolve their sorrow. Grieving as a family or community can move the process along so that grievers can avoid prolonged suffering.

When grief is accompanied by shock, it is more complex. With Rachel, two clues indicated that she had experienced shock: 1) the suddenness of her kitten's death, and 2) her unusual "head-dunking" behavior that followed. For this reason, when I interviewed Rachel I told her that I was curious about why she wanted to dunk her head in water and how this may have helped. Rachel again responded without hesitation: "There was a blood stain on my pants from holding Briar. When I saw it, I was upset and wanted to barf [vomit]. My head was hot. Dunking my head made me feel less upset, not as tense and I wouldn't have to throw up."

Traumatic shock often creates nausea. Seeing blood can be horrible for anyone, especially for kids. It's obvious that Rachel's blood-stained pants triggered another shock reaction. Placing her head in water appeared to have the effect of "soothing her nerves," which settled her tummy. This makes perfect sense from a scientific standpoint. Without getting too technical, it may be helpful for you to know that the vagus nerve travels from the head all the way down to the gut, where it can provoke nausea and reduce blood pressure (producing feelings of faintness) after seeing something gory. Remember that Rachel saw Briar's blood; next, she felt like vomiting. The stimulus of the cold water on her face helped to counter this reaction. Placing a hand on your child's tummy until it begins to settle can also prevent unnecessary discomfort. Rachel intuitively used the cool water to self-soothe as her compassionate parents stood by, letting her lead the way.

Steps That Help Children Resolve Their Grief

Besides moving through sensations of shock and the emotions of grief, there are a few tasks to be completed by the child before saying "good-bye" to his or her loved one. Recall how Rachel needed to "get it off her chest" that she felt sorry she had held Briar even when the kitten clearly didn't like it, and she feared Briar might not have felt she was in a "good home" because of this. Saying what you wish you had done (or not done) is part of releasing yourself from a loved one—whether it's a pet or a person.

EXERCISE: GRIEF RECOVERY

This five-part exercise helps a child take the steps that are a prelude to letting go. The directions are meant to be read by the parent to your child. It is suggested that you work with only one part at a time or even a bit less, depending on your child's tolerance level.

Note: This exercise is modeled after the Grief Recovery Institute's Program, founded by John W. James and Russell Friedman in Sherman Oaks, California, and discussed in their book, *When Children Grieve* (see bibliography).[8]

Part A

1. Make a timeline starting from the date you first met that person or pet until their death.
2. Write several happy memories that stand out as highlights of your relationship above the horizontal timeline in chronological order.
3. Add a few things above the line that you truly appreciated and wish you had told your loved one when he or she was still alive.
4. Write below the line several things that your loved one did that upset you.
5. Add several regrets below the line for things you did that upset your loved one.

Part B

List the memories you wrote under the following headings:

- Things I miss about my loved one
- Things that hurt me that I'd like to forgive now
- Things I feel guilty about that I'd like to be forgiven for
- Things that I appreciated and never said aloud or frequently enough

Part C
Sharing Your Thoughts, Memories and Feelings
Share the lists you made with someone who loves you and will understand. Ask this person or group of people to help you by listening to any feelings that may surface as you complete this set of exercises.

Part D
Saying Good-bye
When you feel ready, compose a special letter for your loved one. Use the memories you listed to express anything you want to say. Don't hold back. It is valuable to balance your letter with things that helped you and things that hurt you. Express gratitude for experiences and feelings that you wish to say "thank you" for. Be open to your shortcomings and theirs. Forgive anything that you feel you want to forgive. Be honest. Don't force yourself to forgive certain things that you don't want to, but be sure to take this opportunity to forgive the things you do. Most of all, forgive yourself. Ask your loved one to forgive you for anything you feel ashamed of and wish you didn't do. Now is the time to come clean so that you can say good-bye without anything holding you back.

This letter can be very hard to write. Have someone you love help you if you cannot do it yourself. But be sure to express your own thoughts and feelings, not someone else's. If you are too young to write all those big words, you can have an older person write your words for you. If you can do it all by yourself, you might want a friend or relative to keep you company in case you have strong feelings that come up. You might want a hug, or someone to hold you if you cry or someone to share your memories and feelings with. In the final line of your letter you tell your loved one "good-bye."

Part E
Sharing Your Letter

When you feel ready, read your good-bye letter to your loved one aloud in front of someone you can trust with your private thoughts and feelings. Then you might want to have a ceremony and bury or burn your letter. Or you might have some very creative ideas of your own to complete the process of grieving.

Giving Emotional Support through the Tears, Fears, Outbursts and Confusion of Grief

Whether children are grieving a death, divorce, separation or loss of some other kind, you can be assured that they will be experiencing a range of different emotions. Young children may not have labels for their feelings. Older children and adolescents may not want to talk about them. It can be very useful to have them draw their feelings instead. One activity that is particularly helpful for kids who are grieving is the "gingerbread person" exercise. After the sketch and color code are finished, the child simply fills in the outline with the various colors to show how they feel in different parts of their body. For example, they might color the entire person blue if they are extremely sad; or they might color the heart area blue, the feet and hands red, and the tummy yellow. (Please see gingerbread person example and directions under "Sensation Body Map" in Chapter III for this and other drawing activities.)

Drawings like this help in two ways: 1) The sensorimotor act of drawing helps to relieve the feelings through artistic expression as it engages the intuitive right side of the brain; and 2) The process gives you, the adult, valuable information about what's troubling your child and what feelings still need to be expressed and listened to with compassion.

Sometimes children will draw their uncomfortable emotions first. As they start feeling better, they may shift and draw pleasant feelings that indicate their natural resilience and resourcefulness. Feelings can be worked through using clay and paints as well. Clay or play dough is especially good for expressing anger, since it can be pounded on, rolled and reshaped any way the child wishes.

Feelings Are a Natural Part of Grieving

Often children (and adults!) are embarrassed about their feelings. They might also try to hide them because they do not want to cause their parents additional pain. This is especially true in the case of divorce or when a sibling, spouse or grandparent dies. As is often the case, the parent(s) may be going through their own painful emotions. It's OK for adults to cry together with their children. In fact, it's important to tell your children that tears, fears and anger are a normal part of the grieving process. Modeling your own healthy emotions without embarrassment can help. Crying tears can release a great deal of pain and stress.

It is critical, however, that you not burden your children with your ongoing suffering or overwhelming feelings of anxiety, depression, rage or sobbing (extremes do not bring relief). Get help from friends and/or counselors if your own grief is not resolving. Refrain from judging or making disparaging remarks about the parent who has left in front of your child. It will confuse him about his own loving feelings for that person.

It is important to ask your child often how she feels and what she thinks. Children may have very different feelings than adults do. Children sense emotions at a primary level (they don't focus on *why* or whether they *should* be feeling something), while adults tend to *analyze* their feelings with an overlay of judgment. Children need to be able to express authentic emotions without having to filter them through an adult lens. They also need to feel safe enough to ask questions on their own timetable. Sometimes children aren't ready to talk about their emotions. Try again later, giving them many opportunities to share with you and unload their burdens when they wish.

Many adults find it easy to hug and comfort a sad child, but find it difficult to deal with a mad one. It is normal to get mad when someone you love leaves. It's important to let children know that mad feelings are normal, too. They may need to talk about it, stomp their feet, draw or write about it, tear up some paper or take a walk. Some children may want to be left alone for a while to work through their feelings on their own or talk with peers. This is especially true for teens. Just let them know that you are available to them *when they are ready.*

Children become afraid when they don't know what's going to happen next. Whether a child is about to move or his parents are about to divorce, he needs to know how he will be affected. You can avoid a lot of catastrophic worry by providing the details of how your child can continue contact by phone, mail and visits with relatives that are still in their lives. In the case of divorce, it helps children to know where they will live, what circumstances will change and which ones will remain the same. Providing telephone numbers, addresses and stationery (or e-mail) to encourage connections can help your child feel more at ease. Encouraging calls to grandparents, aunts, uncles, cousins, etc., on both sides of the family is important. Keeping a connection with extended families often gives kids a sense of continuity that helps them cope better.

Life Will Get Better!

When children's lives go through upheaval, they may ask hundreds of questions in hundreds of ways. "Why can't Dad live with us?" "Why did Grandma have to die?" "Why did Mom leave?" "Will she come back?" "Why can't things be different?" You may not be able to answer every question. But reassuring your child that you are aware of his sadness, frustration, hurt, anger, etc., and that you are right there to listen, hold him, tell him a story or plan ways to make his new life as comfortable as possible can aid your child in the process of grieving and accepting such life-changing losses.

When children are dealing with difficult life transitions, they need to know that life *will get better* with time; things do shift and get easier. It's a delicate balance between supporting your child to express difficult emotions while conveying the sense that "it won't hurt forever." One thing you can do is a regular "feelings check-in" as a daily or weekly ritual to see how emotions begin to change with time. Parents can also hold regular family meetings to share new feelings that come up and check to see how each family member is handling their new situation.

Even when Mom and Dad are with new partners, they need to remain sensitive, responsible co-parents. The emphasis can be on listening compassionately to each other's feelings and problem-solving ways to help their kids manage. This caring and planning makes a huge difference in how well children adjust. Suggestions for family fun-time can also be made during these special gatherings. It's important for children to have a balance between grieving and growing up, which means planning plenty of time for outings, fun, frolic and joy!

CHAPTER VIII

Guerrilla Warfare in Our Neighborhoods: The *Real* Battle to Protect Kids from Terror

> You say you want a revolution
> Well, you know ... we all want to change the world
> You ask me for a contribution ...
> Well, you know we are doing what we can
> We all want to change the institution
> Well, here's the plan ...
>
> *– Inspired by the spirit of*
> *John Lennon* (Imagine *album*)

We have chosen the words "guerrilla warfare" for the title of our final chapter with a bit of tongue-in-cheek. We are by no means implying sabotage, such as a "taking by force" of our existing establishments. The Spanish word "guerrilla" literally means "little war," and those who engage at this level are an independent group fighting to make vital changes. Our founding fathers were true guerrilla heroes when they fought in the Revolutionary War for the freedoms we enjoy today.

We conclude this book with an optimistic look toward the future. We are hoping that what you, the parents, have learned so far will provide an impetus for taking your new knowledge out into your own communities, becoming genuine revolutionaries. Little changes in our society's institutions can make a huge leap forward in the prevention and healing of childhood trauma. Parents can conduct this battle for transformation on two fronts to make our world a healthier and more child-friendly place:

Hospitals and Medical Centers

Community and School Crisis Intervention

Parents might, for instance, become activists organizing grass-roots campaigns in hospitals, neighborhoods and schools to make them "kid-centered." This means that the emotional and spiritual needs of children and their families become central to the medical mission of these institutions. Certain overwhelming events such as injuries and illnesses, natural disasters, terrorism and school crises cannot be avoided. However, traumatic symptoms and debilitating stress for our kids can be greatly reduced, and sometimes even prevented. This chapter makes suggestions for you, the "parent warriors," to bring to your local hospitals, community centers and schools. Keeping our kids resilient is the best antidote for taking the "terror" out of terrorism, regardless of the origin of our children's terrifying experiences.

Models for Change in Hospitals and Medical Centers

Peter's Story

My "career" in developing Somatic Experiencing® began in 1969 when I was asked to treat a woman named Nancy who suffered with a myriad of physical problems including migraines, a painful condition that would now be called fibromyalgia, chronic fatigue, severe PMS and irritable bowel syndrome, as well as various "psychological" problems including frequent panic attacks. During this session (described in *Waking the Tiger: Healing Trauma*) Nancy began to tremble, shake and sob in waves of full-body convulsions. For almost an hour she continued to shake as she recalled terrifying images and feelings from age four. She had been held down by doctors and nurses and struggled in vain during a tonsillectomy with ether anesthesia.

As I worked with more and more people with symptoms like Nancy's, I was shocked at how many had similar experiences as young children, during which they were overwhelmed and terrified by invasive medical procedures. As I began to train people in the method I was developing, I also got to confront my own terrifying tonsillectomy. Like Nancy, I struggled against the doctors and nurses who held me down. Desperately I tried to escape the terror of suffocation, but was overpowered and overwhelmed with panic and utter helplessness. As I worked through this experience, feelings of fearfulness, "tummy aches" and betrayal that had plagued me throughout my adult life loosened their grip. Both Nancy and I re-owned an innocence and vitality that had been cruelly, though unintentionally, taken from us during early childhood.

It was at that point I felt propelled to do what I could to prevent children from becoming unnecessarily traumatized. And while hospitals have come a long way since the 1940s and '50s, when Nancy and I had our tonsillectomies, even simple medical procedures performed on children are still often experienced as frightening, painful and overwhelming—as we learned with Sammy in Chapter III.

The "war on terror" can begin by reducing the suffering endured by children unnecessarily and inflicted inadvertently by the health care system. Doctors, nurses and allied professionals are in the business of saving lives. Devoted staff members often suffer "burnout," or vicarious trauma, as they deal (day in and day out) with catastrophic illnesses, injuries and what is often a chaotic, frenzied environment. Add to that the "managed care" bureaucracy that can bury both health care providers and patients in paperwork. Is it really surprising that precious little time has been given thus far to consider a different approach that might reduce, minimize or eliminate traumatic reactions after the operation is over?

Medical and surgical procedures are supposed to resolve patients' health problems—not create new ones. Whether interventions are urgent or planned, dealing with them can be difficult, even for adults. More often than not the procedures are tricky and frightening, not to mention potentially harmful, as one can see when asked to sign the cautionary forms prior to treatment. Ideally, with the suggestions presented in this final chapter, you, the parents, will be motivated to participate in creating positive change.

Although the responsibility to provide care that prevents unnecessary suffering, facilitates quicker recovery time, prevents future trauma symptoms and saves money lies in the hands of medical personnel and administrators, we live in a business-driven environment. Therefore, you, as the consumers of health care for your family, often have the power that comes with patronage. Any health care facility can readily implement the ideas presented here. Parents and medical staff together, united in their vision to improve pediatric medical care, can be powerful allies in bringing a new consciousness to our systems of care. This new direction would be best if it added a stress prevention program to its existing model. With humanistic practices incorporated system-wide, the following benefits can be expected:

- Children who might otherwise suffer following terrifying medical procedures will have a chance to grow up healthy and resilient.

- These same children as adults later in life may be less saddled with anxiety and other psychological, physical and medical symptoms of trauma. They may be more likely to rebound in the aftermath of overwhelming experiences, because a predisposition for hopelessness and helplessness has not been imprinted.

- Children who are surgical patients would have the possibility of a quicker recovery time.

- Serious health problems, and even some violent acts, might be averted.

- The needs of the body, mind and spirit could share more equal weight in patient planning decisions, giving children the respect and dignity they deserve.

- Society might save incalculable sums of money in health care costs, not to mention the alleviation of much human suffering.

Currently, many hospitals and medical centers provide excellent treatment, saving lives that previously would have been lost. The next step is to provide immediate, effective interventions to address mental, emotional and spiritual issues.

One such hospital that is beginning to examine the value of services that address the emotional aspects of a patient's experience is the Children's Hospital of the University of California at San Francisco Medical Center. In an exciting collaboration with both the Pediatric Rheumatology and Rehabilitation Medicine Divisions along with two members of the Child Life Department, Karen Schanche (a pediatric social worker) has developed and implemented an innovative treatment program for pediatric patients. This program is designed to reduce symptoms associated with various medical treatments.[2]

Karen, a former student of ours, has been using Somatic Experiencing® principles with both outpatients and inpatients under her care. She prepares children (four to eighteen years of age) who are in the rheumatology outpatient program to successfully cope with multiple painful joint injections during regular clinic visits without having to undergo general anesthesia. In addition to showing them how the procedure will affect them, she spends time with the children to determine what they need to feel safe and comfortable, introduces them to sensations, role-plays with making boundaries and helps them find ways to access inner resources in order to maintain a sense of some control. Part of this process includes empowering the children to make decisions about *who* they want with them and *how* they want that person to be involved in helping them manage the sensations of pressure and pain during the procedure.

As these young patients use such techniques as switching their focus from painful sensations to pleasurable (or at least less painful) ones, they are more prepared to endure the pain with minimal discomfort. This allows them to surrender to their sensations, reducing the pain and anguish of the injections while maintaining a sense of control and larger purpose. Karen reports the almost magical result that the majority of children are much more cooperative when receiving these injections with support, compared to when they have to undergo general anesthesia. She said that kids have made comments like "I'm not feeling nauseated and I don't have to throw up!" The children, generally, are amazed at how much better they feel without the anesthesia.

The biggest bonus is that the children are free of the psychological and physical complications that come from being restrained and drugged. Embla numbing cream and freezing spray are applied locally instead of sedation. Rather than the children feeling helpless as they are held down to experience excruciating pain, Karen empowers the children by helping them to feel their protective responses and strength by using "push hands" or "push away" games. Some of these pushing and pressure exercises can be done during the injections to distract the young patients as they focus on the sensations of using their own powerful muscles. Karen often integrates Somatic Experiencing® with techniques that use the child's own imagery and metaphor. To date, she has prepared twenty-seven children who are in treatment in the outpatient Rheumatology Program and seven inpatient rehabilitation patients. The child patients are appreciative, and the doctors appear impressed by the improvement in their pediatric patient satisfaction and ability to handle stressful medical procedures with less distress.

While much more research is needed on approaches such as the one at UCSF Medical Center, we (the authors) have noted from anecdotal reports that individuals who receive Somatic Experiencing® treatments before and after medical procedures usually testify to rapid recovery. This includes symptomatic relief and an ability to return to a "full life," even after serious procedures.

A Peek at a Model Family-Centered Children's Hospital

Although few in number, attitudes and environments are being created that are sensitive and humane. Some hospitals working to minimize pediatric trauma are those funded by the Make-A-Wish Foundation.[3] Let's look at what they are doing to prevent trauma and make a child's hospital stay more pleasant and less scary.

One such forward-looking hospital is Miller Children's Hospital at Long Beach Memorial Medical Center in California. Directions given by Rita, the manager of the Child Life Program, to find the Center were heartening: "Enter by the blue dolphin and go straight to the boat, where you will find a receptionist to give you a visitor badge." Her warm welcoming tone gave a feeling of comfort and nurturance even before starting the tour of this remarkable pediatric unit. This hospital's commitment to the total care of each child extends to the whole family. Both child and parents are oriented about what to expect before, during and after the medical procedures. When appropriate, the Sibling Program prepares brothers and sisters for their first hospital visit as well.

The Child Life Program was developed with the sole purpose of making the hospital experience a positive one for both outpatient and inpatient kids. Child Life Specialists plan individualized and group programs that familiarize children with what to expect from their hospital experience in a way that helps lessen fear and anxiety. They use simulated equipment, books and "Jeffrey," the life-sized doll dressed in child-friendly hospital pajamas and blue surgical cap. "Jeffrey" has a special box with EKG stickers, a pulsometer, an IV, a blood pressure cuff and a syringe that children get to look at, feel and play with. Next, each child is shown a book with photos that orient her to the hospital experience step by step. Kids get involved at the start by picking out the color of some very cool pajamas (with little bears and stars) and slippers that they can keep.

I got to witness the program in action with Daniel, a little boy who was about to have a mass removed from his neck. He listened spellbound to the story that the Child Life Specialist read to him. Next, Daniel got to touch the EKG stickers that the Specialist said were "sticky on the outside and gooey in the middle." After he played with them, she demonstrated for Daniel exactly how they would be placed on his chest and showed him a photo of another child getting the same stickers.

This orientation took place in the playroom, which was equipped with carpeted climbing stairs, a slide and a television theater featuring shows like "Bear and the Big Blue House." The episode playing while Daniel was being prepped was about "Doc Hog's visit to the big blue house to examine bear and all of his friends." After the preparation, Daniel got to play on the slide with his mom and dad until the doctor came to meet his family. When the doctor arrived, he played a few minutes with Daniel so that he would not be a stranger. Next, he patiently answered any questions the family had. He also explained the sequence of events in simple language.

At Miller, children are given their own doll to dress up in pajamas, along with a medical play kit containing a mask, syringe, gloves, cotton, alcohol swab, band-aid, tongue depressor and a medicine cup. There are coloring books with titles such as "Tommy's [the Turtle] Trip to MRI" and "My Hospital Book," as well as a library of videos, books and medical Internet access for parents and teens. Children are given a tour of the play-rooms they will get to spend time enjoying after their treatments in order to tantalize them with something to look forward to while recuperating.

Miller Children's also incorporates state-of-the-art pain-reducing technology. For example, they have "patient-controlled analgesic" machines that operate by a push of a button. It is so safe and sim-ple that children as young as five years old can operate one! They are controlled in such a way that it is impossible for a child to over-dose on the medication while at the same time getting sufficient pain alleviation.

A non-drug pain reliever is the mobile "Fun Center" complete with TV, VCR and interactive video games. The Child Life Program manager shared that a study conducted by the University of South-ern California in Los Angeles using these play stations monitored physiological reactions of young sickle-cell patients experiencing a pain crisis. Research results were conclusive in finding signifi-cantly reduced pain responses in children who were given the opportunity to use the "Fun Center." A benefit is that it can be used by both children and adolescents. Another program that works especially well with teens (and children of all ages who may not have actively involved parents) is "The Grandparent Program." This core of volunteers plays cards, sits, talks, listens and just spends caring time with the kids, keeping them from getting lonely and bored.

In addition to the Child Life Program, great care has been taken to make Miller Children's Hospital a delightful environment for kids. Each room has a colorful mural with an ocean theme. Little kids get to be surrounded by lots of sea creatures, while teens have scenes like surfboards in the sand. There are bedside games, pet visitations and elaborate playrooms. The playrooms offer every-thing from arts, crafts and imaginative play to special video confer-encing through "Starbright World," a health care organization that connects children interactively online to other children, internationally, having a similar medical condition. As if that were not enough, the "Giggles" TV studio broadcasts live daily, with reception available in every room. This show features a child patient, a Child Life Specialist and, of course, "Giggles the Clown"! Other child patients can call in with questions, and everyone who calls wins a prize. The TV "guest" can expect peer visitors who are eager to get an autograph from the patient "star" of the day.

In addition to Child Life Specialists who prepare children and walk them through procedures, there are social workers and psychologists available to help children emotionally who, despite best efforts, may still be having traumatic reactions. Staff is also on the alert to identify children needing specialized help during their recovery period. If this kind of care seems too good to be true, well, maybe this is *exactly how it should be;* furthermore, with our book in hand, you might just find that your local hospital is interested in incorporating some of these very same ideas.

Enhancing Trauma Prevention Efforts

Although there are growing numbers of conscious medical centers doing their best to increase the comfort level of children and create an appealing environment, often the simplest but most important practices to prevent trauma remain unknown or overlooked.

The good news is that pediatric trauma prevention does not require fancy or expensive equipment. The skills to prevent trauma can be made available to everyone. The first step is to educate pediatric medical personnel regarding the physical dynamics that underlie trauma. Because trauma symptoms come from immobility, helplessness and the energy bound in the thwarted flight-or-fight response, it is essential *to make absolutely sure that no child is strapped down and subjected to being anesthetized in a terrified state.*

Doctors, nurses, social workers and Child Life Specialists need to be alert to a child's feelings and strive to lessen anxiety. The child's reactions should be closely monitored. Body language and facial expressions often tell the story of a child's fears better than words (i.e., with a "deer-in-the headlights" frozen expression). Frequently, children are terrified "speechless." It is usually best if the orientation to the hospital routine and the role-playing can happen the week before, rather than on the day of the surgery, so that parents can be taught to play "hospital" at home until the child is comfortable enough to cooperate.

Another very important point in trauma prevention, mentioned earlier in Chapter IV, cannot be overstated. When a child must undergo surgery, *it is important for a local anesthetic to be administered along the line of incision* whenever possible. Currently this is not routinely done despite a growing body of research indicating that the local anesthetic improves the rate of recovery and lessens complications.[4] Many times a local can be given without the potential risks of a general anesthesia; however, a general should not be given without a local in many cases. In addition to quicker recovery time, there is another benefit of administering a local anesthetic. Because the body still registers the point of surgical incision as an invasion when only a general anesthesia is given (perhaps no different than that of a vicious animal attack), adding a local anesthetic along the cut can aid in leaving a child feeling less vulnerable, therefore less susceptible to later psychological symptoms.

Taking Good Programs to the Next Level of Trauma Intervention

Miller Children's Hospital at Long Beach Memorial Medical Center is one of a network of ninety model hospitals in the United States that are family-friendly. By adding the simple but crucial recommendations described above it would be very easy to initiate change in programs such as these that put children's needs first. All it would take is for parents to educate their local hospital staff regarding the principles of trauma prevention outlined in this book. Be sure to choose a facility that understands the crucial importance of preventing medical trauma through sensitive practices, orientation and preparation. It is also vital to choose a medical center or hospital that is willing to work as a team with parents. Contact www.ChildLifeCouncil.org to learn more about bringing programs such as Child Life and Make-A-Wish to your community. Be pro-active in reminding them, however, that *sophisticated equipment is not the essential ingredient of a trauma-prevention/ stress reduction program.* Understanding and alleviating children's fear, worry and pain is the true hallmark of prevention. Remember that the medical staff is supposed to serve your child and family—not the other way around! Know, and insist, on your family's rights. Ultimately it is up to you to make choices that make change happen!

CANDI'S STORY

Candi is a young Child Life Specialist intern whom I met when I visited Miller Children's Hospital. She was especially curious about our work in trauma prevention and captured my attention with her enthusiasm for her career. I listened intently to her story. Candi described her younger self as an outgoing, friendly little girl who was also a dancer. When she was seven years old she noticed a mysterious and debilitating pain in her knee requiring medical attention. Candi said that she will never forget her dreadful and terrifying hospital experience. The doctor was "digging and poking" around her knee until an embedded sewing needle was discovered. But embedded even deeper in her memory were the insensitive words she thought she heard the doctor say to the nurses: "If we can't get the needle out, we may have to cut off the leg."

As an adult Candi said, "I understand that they saved my life—the needle could have traveled to my heart—but I was *SO* scared.

Nothing was done to comfort me. When the ordeal was over, the nurses said, 'Be sure to tell your mom what a great job the nurses did!' But they didn't."

I asked Candi how her hospital experience had affected her life. She told me that she has been shy and anxious ever since that day. She shared that this was her motivation to devote her life to the prevention of medical trauma in children so that no child in her care has to endure that kind of suffering.

Many people experience hospitals and medical clinics as foreign, threatening and even dangerous places. This perceived threat is heightened when a person seeks medical care for a serious health challenge that *is* actually life-threatening. Medical trauma is particularly significant for children. Many adults recall fears of suffocation, immobilization and terror they endured as a result of medical treatment received in childhood.

Fortunately, as you have seen, much can be done to bring more humane care into the medical setting. Through simple modification of approaches, hospital staff can dramatically influence the degree of safety or degree of threat that our kids experience. Orientation, preparation with the use of role-play, help in processing "the bad-news diagnosis" as it is happening and intentional use of positive language are key examples of powerful tools that health care workers can easily employ to improve outcomes for our littlest patients.

Obviously, pediatric professionals need to be trained so that they understand, like you now do, *the nature of trauma*. Our hope is that in the foreseeable future, all hospitals and medical centers will understand the importance of preventing or minimizing stress and shock-trauma in all patients—but particularly our most vulnerable citizens, our children. In the meantime you, the parents, can play a pivotal role in changing the current system by becoming constructive, revolutionary, peaceful warriors of healing, armed and ready with knowledge and compassion.

Community Crisis Intervention

The last several years have brought a quickening effect of tragedy, due in part to increased natural disasters caused by extreme weather, the threat of new diseases, school shootings, pervasive media coverage of violence and the advent of terrorism on American soil. This section is for parents who wish to be fortified with more skills to help kids cope in the wake of community catastrophes and mass fatalities. The ideas and activities described in this section can be used by grassroots community organizers with groups of children. They are appropriate for a variety of events that can shake a neighborhood, from the atrocities mentioned above, to accidental multiple deaths such as a mining disaster, to a classmate's suicide. The principles of emotional first aid that you have learned thus far can also be applied equally in the case of natural disasters such as fire, hurricanes, earthquakes, tornadoes, floods and tsunamis.

Before disaster strikes it is important for ordinary people to come together as a core of volunteers with a school or neighborhood plan that can be implemented when necessary to comfort and help one another and assist those children and adults who remain numb with shock and terror. If you, the parents, have an action plan it is less likely that you will give in to the temptation to stay isolated at home, perhaps being mesmerized into watching the horror repeatedly on the news in your own state of shock. Together, parents can help their kids bounce back as quickly as possible from the disruption of their daily routines.

Our New Reality

On September 11, 2001, the collective reality of safety was shattered in the United States. It is likely that similar events will occur again. We were left with profound, unanswered questions and fears about what might happen next and what to tell our children. In fact, more important than *what* we say is *how* we speak with them about such horrible things and *how we listen* to their feelings and concerns. Children take more from the feelings of their parents than from their words. Their needs have less to do with information and more with security. Children need to know that they are protected and loved. The words "I love you and will protect you"—spoken from the heart—mean more than any kind of explanation. Young children need to be communicated with through physical contact, holding, rocking and touch.

In families where both parents work, it is important to take time to phone your young child so that she knows you are still there. Predictability and the continuity of keeping a routine are important for children of all ages. The making of plans together to give them a sense that life will go on and that they will have fun again is another important thing we can do to alleviate distress for our children.

Because the media use graphic fear as a selling point, it is important to minimize children's TV news exposure—particularly during dinner and before bedtime. Of course, it's best to watch the news after they are asleep. Kids three to five years of age may ask questions about things that they have heard or seen on TV. At these ages children are beginning to be able to put feelings into words, and you can let them know that it is OK to have these feelings. Drawing pictures and talking about what they have drawn and how it makes them feel can be helpful, as can the telling of stories where the hero/heroine has overcome difficult situations and been made stronger by meeting and mastering an ordeal.

In addition, children will often draw some new creative element in their pictures to help them contextualize what has happened. For example, one child who witnessed the planes crash into the World Trade Center and then saw people jumping out of the windows drew the scene but with one significant addition—he drew a small round object on the ground. When asked by his parents what it was, he replied, "It's a trampoline to help save the people falling out of the windows."

For older children, six to twelve years of age, more direct discussions can be held. It may be important to find out where they
got their information and what their specific fears are. Then you
can have the family brainstorm ideas for things that they can do
to help the people who have been affected, such as sending letters
to the children who lost loved ones or organizing a fund-raiser to
collect aid money. Mobilizing helpful activity, rather than being a
spectator, can make a big difference.

Mass Disaster Assistance Lacking for Families and Communities after 9/11

American Red Cross Disaster Mental Health Coordinator Lisa
LaDue (then Senior Advisor for the National Mass Fatalities Institute[5]) was assigned to the Red Cross Headquarters in Arlington,
Virginia, following the 9/11 attack on the Pentagon. Her job was
to respond to requests from the metropolitan Washington, DC,
community for debriefings, consultations and counseling. This is
what she told us during an interview in 2006:

> The common cry echoed from parents and community lead-
> ers was unequivocally the same: "We need help so we can
> help our children." It was quite clear that most people were
> at a great loss to know how to help kids recover from this
> disaster. Parents were afraid to take their children to school;
> children were afraid when their parents went to work or
> even to the store. Whole neighborhoods were afraid to leave
> their homes after dark. No one seemed to know how to
> address the effects of terror. These incidents clearly illus-
> trate the need for coordinated services to help children and
> adults regain their equilibrium in order to recover from both
> direct and vicarious trauma.

> Parents can become community leaders or directors of volun-
> tary organizations that address the terror of terrorism and other

mass disasters (man-made or natural). Somatic Experiencing® offers hope in restoring a sense of safety for the children and their families. It provides a fresh approach in recovering from events that shake us collectively as human beings. Armed with new knowledge of how to respond, parents can organize simple games with the neighborhood kids that allow discharge of the traumatic energy. You might also teach them how to integrate art, writing and other expressive forms with body sensation awareness to help calm and settle their nervous systems. Rather than be exasperated with feelings of helplessness because your children are having difficulty sleeping or are afraid to leave home, you can offer these simple somatic tools to restore a sense of balance to their lives.

A child's fearful face, a classroom with children demonstrating regressive, disruptive behavior and families who find their children lacking the energy to enjoy life the way they did before are all loud warning bells beckoning us to come forth with a grassroots plan for neighborhoods and schools that addresses the crux of trauma in order to restore resilience as rapidly as possible.

Restoring the Resilience of Kids after Natural Disasters: Lessons from Thailand

Using the tools of working with trauma described in this book, the Trauma Outreach Program (TOP) team, made up of a group of Somatic Experiencing® Practitioners, worked and played with school children in Thailand after the historic December 2004 Indian Ocean earthquake caused a devastating tsunami. Another group of Somatic Experiencing® Practitioners, Trauma Vidya, led by Raja Selvam, helped survivors in southern India. Both teams worked to help kids, parents and teachers recover from the horrible shock and grief of watching families, homes, sources of livelihood and animals suddenly being swept away. Workshops were given on the principles of trauma first aid to build the capacity of local people to continue the relief work long after our teams returned home. The following guidelines and games will prepare you to help groups of children in your own community bounce back if a disaster were to strike.

Because trauma overwhelms the nervous system, kids who have experienced trauma often have difficulty feeling confident, balanced and in control of their behavior. They may be hyperactive, demonstrating poor impulse control, or they may be lethargic, spacey or depressed. In order to help these kids, any familiar game such as "capture the flag" and jump rope can be adapted to incorporate the simple principles of body awareness that you have already learned. The excitement and competition provoked by these physical activities arouse a similar energy to those used for fight/flight responses. The group activities will also help you to see how your child and other neighborhood kids you care about are coping.

Activities need to be structured so that highly energized periods of excitation are interspersed with equal periods of rest to give kids sufficient time for settling down. During the time set aside for settling—which can be accomplished by having them sit quietly in a circle—the parent leader does a sensation "check-in" to see how the kids are feeling. In groups it's easiest to ask for a show of hands, using questions such as: Who feels strong now? Who feels weak? Who has energy? Who feels tired? Who feels hot? Who feels cold? Who feels calm? Who feels sick? Who feels excited? Whose heart is beating fast? Who feels power in their legs? Who has a headache or bellyache? Who feels happy?

During both phases (the excitement and the settling), excess energy is automatically discharged. As children "chase," "flee," "escape" and feel vigor and power in their arms, legs and trunk, they are strengthening the centers in the brain that support resiliency and self-regulation. Sensory experiences through play help kids to regain their confidence and stamina. When children are encouraged in this way to heighten awareness of their body states, it is much easier to restore resilience after a mishap.

Suggested Group Activities that Foster Connection and Resilience

We used several games with school-aged kids in Thailand to help them regain confidence and resilience after the devastating tsunami altered their lives forever. The "Coyote (or Tiger) Chases Rabbit" game, "Pretend Jump Rope" and several other activities were successful in helping children discharge some of their anxiety while having fun. Some who complained of headache, weakness in their legs and/or stomachache (or who appeared depressed or anxious) started to recover their vitality as they began to experience mastery through team play. Watching the children's limp bodies come to life and their sad faces light up with laughter and joy was a sublime experience. Some of the kids, more traumatized than others, needed individualized adult support in order to fully participate. Instructions are provided later in this section on how parents can give each child the extra assistance he or she may need.

COYOTE CHASES RABBIT

This game and the next one use the principles of Somatic Experiencing® and were designed for groups by our colleague Alexandre Duarte, who did trauma relief work with children in Thailand, India, New Orleans and Baton Rouge. We called this game "Tiger Chases Rabbit" in Asia since the tiger is an animal that local children are familiar with. Obviously you can vary the critters while the essential game remains the same. For this activity all that is needed are two balls of different colors and sizes. This game is designed to simulate the flight response. Parents from the neighborhood or volunteer parents, teachers and counselors at school can rally to help the kids after a disaster.

To start, the adults and children form a standing circle and then sit on the floor in that arrangement. The leader holds up one ball, saying, "This is the rabbit." Then the rabbit gets passed around the circle hand to hand, starting off slowly. The adults encourage the kids to gradually increase the pace.

Soon participants begin to feel their sensations of anticipation grow as the rabbit "runs" from child to child.

A parent then introduces a second ball as Mr. or Ms. Coyote (Tiger, etc.) and starts the second ball chasing the "rabbit." The pace increases naturally as the children identify with the strength of the coyote and the speed of the rabbit, and as the excitement of the chase escalates. The complexity of the game can be increased for older children by calling out a change in direction. The idea is not to win or lose but to feel the excitation of the chase and the power of the team effort to pass the balls quickly so as not to get "caught."

Next, the children rest. As they settle, the leader checks in with them, asking for a show of hands to identify the various sensations they may be feeling. After playing this game for a while, have the group participants stand up and feel their legs and their connection to the ground so that they can discharge activated energy through their bodies. Those children who feel weak or lack energy can get the extra support they need from an adult. For example, you might have the less energetic kids pretend they are bunnies; the adults hold their hands while helping them to hop by sharing their stamina and enthusiasm and seeing how high they can get them to hop, first with assistance and then on their own.

At the end of the play period, children need to be monitored carefully to make sure that no one is frozen or shut down. If a child is rigid or spacey, an adult might do a grounding exercise with him until he becomes more present. "Push hands"—where the parent can give a little resistance while a child pushes his own hands against the adult's—can also be helpful in getting a child settled into the present moment.

THE PRETEND JUMP ROPE

This game gives kids an opportunity to run toward (rather than away from) something that creates activation and to experience a successful escape. No jump rope is needed. This game is done as a pantomime. Two children or adults hold a pretend jump rope while the others line up for a turn just like in regular jump rope. First the rope is swung back and forth at a low level near the ground. You can increase the imaginary height if the child seems to desire more challenge. One by one students jump over the "rope" to safety. The reason for not using an actual jump rope is that the lack of a real one engages the imagination and reduces the likelihood of falling. It symbolizes a manageable threat coming toward them. This elicits spontaneous movements and gives children the satisfaction of a successful escape.

Note: More group activities that parents can use together with neighbors or teachers, such as "The Empowerment Game," "The Wolf Comes at Midnight," "Past-Present-Future Hopscotch" and "Parachute" activities can be found in Chapters Eleven and Twelve of *Trauma Through A Child's Eyes: Awakening the Ordinary Miracle of Healing.*

Note for Physical Activities

The key to "assisted self-regulation" after a disaster is the presence of adult activity leaders who are able to assess and assist those kids having difficulty. While some youngsters will have trouble settling down (they will not be hard to spot!), others will recede to the shadows or complain of being too tired to continue or having a headache, tummy ache, etc. For the children who are struggling, the adults need to be skillful in dealing with their special needs. Here's where extra help comes in handy. These activities are best carried out with several other grown-ups co-facilitating to ensure that every child who needs assistance gets it.

When some kids need extra help to feel successful, the leaders model for the whole group how to support each other in learning self-regulation. For example, a student complaining of fatigue during the sensation "check-in" might lie down and rest her head on the lap or shoulder of a friendly teacher or classmate, while another adult helps her explore where she feels tired. If she says, "my legs," the child can rest the legs for a bit and later be given support to move her legs slowly when ready—perhaps pretending she is moving like her favorite animal. This may include physically helping the child to move her legs alternately while lying on her back with knees up and feet flat on a mat.

For the child who is hyperactive and needing help to settle, an adult or more regulated student can sit next to her, helping her to feel the ground and to inhale and exhale more slowly. A partner or an adult might place a firm hand on the student's shoulder or back as he grounds himself, communicating calmness through contact. The main idea is to normalize individual differences and teach the group how to help one another as they connect more deeply.

It Takes a Village: Katrina, Rita and Other Natural Disasters

With the comfort of home washed away and families torn apart by the Gulf Coast hurricanes of 2005, school staff were being challenged, perhaps for the first time, to help pupils muddle through the aftermath of disaster. In an article entitled "Helping Students Cope with a Katrina-Tossed World" (*The New York Times*, November 16, 2005), Emma Daly reported that elementary school students in Gulfport, Mississippi, kept coming to see the school nurse at Three Rivers Elementary School "with vague complaints: headaches or stomach pains that are rarely accompanied by fevers or other symptoms." (Actually, children will sometimes have fevers in the aftermath of loss and trauma.) Other pupils were quiet and withdrawn. All of these symptoms, of course, are common in post-disaster situations. Most people, however, don't connect physical symptoms to trauma. Dr. Lynne Jones, advisor to the International Medical Corps regarding hurricane-affected populations, is quoted in the same newspaper story as emphasizing the importance of normalizing symptoms by saying something to the children like, "This is to be expected; if you have been through a very frightening, painful experience, the pain and fear settle in part of your body." It is precisely because the body does bear the burden that the model throughout this book for the *prevention* of long-term trauma involves helping kids notice and work through their body's sensations and feelings painlessly. Games "with a twist" that promote a charge and discharge of energy, together with the sharing of sensations and feelings, restore a sense of pleasure and competency, replacing feelings of helplessness and hopelessness.

In natural disasters and other mass-fatality situations, like terrorist attacks and war, the local caregivers are personally affected as well. "Mass disasters produce a peculiar reticence in grief—everybody is looking after everybody else," continues Dr. Jones. Everybody has lost something, so the tendency is to suffer silently rather than burden your neighbor. In Thailand, for example, a mother who had lost one child had a friend who lost all of her children and her house. The mother told us she felt that she shouldn't hurt as bad as she did because her friend lost even more! But such inequities of loss don't mean that one's own pain or trauma is diminished. Children are especially protective, trying to spare parents any sorrow because they need to see them as able to cope. Kids often keep their pain secret in an attempt to relieve their parents' distress.

For this reason group support is essential for both parents and children to counteract the tendency toward withdrawal and isolation. If neighbors come together in emergency preparedness efforts such as with their friends from "Neighborhood Watch," they can practice the skills and the games in advance. This way they can generate a plan for meeting together with their kids to support them and each other following a catastrophe. Neighbors need neighbors. People heal people!

A New Model of Crisis Debriefing at School

Traditional crisis intervention in the schools typically is designed to debunk myths, get everyone on the same page with the facts, normalize traumatic reactions and give the children a chance to talk about what happened. The debriefing team might even ask the kids to tell about the worst parts of what they saw and how they feel; then, off they go!

There is little if any processing (working through) of the awful experiences they were asked to describe! We, the authors, believe that such debriefing with a lack of integration can be re-traumatizing, especially for children. And because children (and many traumatized adults as well) tend to be compliant, the first responder *may not be aware* that the child is being pushed further into shutdown and dissociation.

Somatic Experiencing® offers a new model for crisis intervention in the school and community. It was used successfully with Thai children in the aftermath of the 2004 tsunami and with survivors of Hurricanes Katrina and Rita in the United States. Those treated in New Orleans, Baton Rouge and Thailand participated in a research study that demonstrated dramatic benefits in both the short and long term. A significant reduction in trauma symptoms was evident after only one to two Somatic Experiencing® "first aid" sessions.

The Critical Difference in Somatic Experiencing® Crisis Intervention

The emphasis in Somatic Experiencing® "first aid" is on symptom relief and in resolving the underlying "energy" that feeds those symptoms. This is accomplished by assisting children to reduce excess nervous system arousal through accessing his or her internal sensation-based resources. This is in sharp contrast to some other methods that focus on gathering and disseminating information and asking kids to describe the catastrophe. Instead, children are asked to share their post-event difficulties—not their memories. Common reactions after a disaster include: eating and sleep disturbances, irritability, spaciness, weakness in the limbs, fatigue, numbness, headaches, feeling dead, flashbacks, worry about the future, panic and survivor's guilt.

Great care is taken to avoid re-traumatization by refraining from probing for the "telling of the story." SE® does not ask grief-stricken, terrified children to talk about "the worst thing that happened." Instead, support is given by observing and listening to each child's bodily reactions and helping them to move out of shock and distress. Sensations and emotions are processed in very small increments. And the child only reveals bits of the story as they arise spontaneously rather than being deliberately provoked.

In the following example you will learn how SE® crisis intervention is conducted. In this case, a group of middle-school students helplessly watched a drive-by shooting as they waited for their bus. The counselor met with the small group later that morning and a few times subsequently. One boy and one girl, however, continued to have problems and were referred for crisis counseling. After using our somatic approach, both youngsters' symptoms resolved. Curtis's story (below) is a poignant example of the details of using Somatic Experiencing® after a crisis.

Restoring Curtis's Innocence after a Drive-By Shooting

Curtis was a middle-school boy who witnessed a drive-by shooting at the bus stop. He was referred by his counselor because he couldn't stop thinking about the event. At school Curtis was restless and distracted; at home he was physically aggressive with his brother. When I met Curtis he told me that he didn't want to act the way he was acting. He "wanted to feel like himself again." He said that his biggest problem was the angry feelings he had each time he pictured the man who was shot lying on the ground. He also got distracted in class and had difficulty sleeping. But he shared that what troubled him the most were the brand-new feelings of wanting to hurt somebody—anybody, any random target—without understanding why.

When I asked where he felt the anger, he said, "In my legs and feet." Together we tracked the sensations in his legs and feet. Within a minute or two of noticing his lower body, Curtis was able to tell me that his legs wanted to kick. He also mentioned that he liked kickball and soccer and described feeling strong in his legs (an important resource). As we worked together, Curtis discovered that he wished he could have kicked the gun out of the gang member's hands. I had Curtis use his legs to kick a soccer ball in the same way he had wanted to kick the gun. He started to kick the ball with vigor.

Rather than have Curtis kick fast and hard, perhaps getting wound up and enraged, I gently showed him how to make the kicking movements in slow motion. I had him describe the sensations in his hips, legs and feet as he prepared to kick (what his body wanted to do to stop the violence). Then I invited Curtis to rest and notice the feelings in his legs. Each time that we followed this sequence, his legs would shake and tremble. Once this activated energy was discharged, Curtis centered himself, took a deep breath and kicked the ball full-out, as he felt his steadiness, strength and confidence return. He got his power back and lost the urge to hurt a random bystander.

After this "first aid" session to move his body out of shock, Curtis's symptoms disappeared. In a follow-up several weeks later with Curtis and the school counselor, he continued to be symptom-free. He was relieved that he no longer felt pointless aggression. Curtis shared that he felt like himself again. Not only did he get his power back; he got his innocence back! The major shift in this type of crisis work is that the focus is not on the horror of the event; rather it is on *completion* of the body's incomplete responses to protect and defend itself and others. This is what led to symptom relief and long-term transformation of trauma for Curtis.

Crisis Relief with Groups

The SE® crisis work done with Curtis could have been done with the entire group of middle-school students had the counselor been trained in working with the principles of tracking sensations, nervous system activation/deactivation and sensorimotor defensive movements. Suggestions that follow are for school-wide trauma first aid after a crisis such as a natural disaster, school shooting or terrorist attack. Parents and educators can partner together to help children calm their aroused states in small groups at school.

As the kids assemble, one student usually volunteers. As she is supported to process her symptoms and gets relief, the shyer students gain confidence and ask for their turn. Below are guidelines for working with groups of three to twelve students:

1. Invite as many parents (or other caregivers) as possible to participate.

2. Seat students in a circle so that everyone can see each other. Seat adults directly behind the children in a concentric circle for support.

3. It is very helpful but not necessary to have a child-size fitness ball for the student who is "working." Sitting on the ball helps youngsters drop into and describe their sensations more easily. These balls are very comfortable and children love to sit on them.

4. Educate the group on the trauma response. Explain what the children might expect to experience both during the initial shock phase and as the shock begins to wear off in order to normalize their symptoms. Use the information that you have learned in this book. (For example, some may feel numb; others may have recurring images or troublesome thoughts, etc.) Explain what you will be doing to help them (i.e., that the group will be learning about inner sensations and how they help to move stuck feelings, images and worrisome thoughts out of their body and mind).

5. Do not probe the group to describe what happened during the event. Instead explain to them that you will teach skills to help lessen symptoms so they might feel some relief.

6. Ask the group to share some of the trauma symptoms they may be having (for example: difficulty sleeping, eating or concentrating; nightmares; feeling that "it didn't really happen"). At the same time it is important not to over-focus on the symptoms; this can have the effect of causing more worry

and may reinforce the feeling that there is something wrong with the person experiencing the symptom(s). Symptoms are only discussed to provide the knowledge that these are normal responses and to help guide children toward balance and equilibrium.

7. Explain what a sensation is (distinguishing it from an emotion) and have the group brainstorm various sensation words. You might even write these down for all to see, if convenient. Explain what to expect: that they might feel trembling or shaking, be tearful, jittery, nauseous, warm, cool, numb; or they might feel like they want to run, fight, disappear or hide. Let the group participants know that these are sensations that can occur as they are moving out of shock.

8. Work with one volunteer at a time within the circle. Have that child notice the support of the adults and other students in the group. Invite him to make eye contact with a special friend or familiar adult for safety. At any time during the session, if the student needs extra support, invite him again to take a break and make contact with a special "buddy" in the group.

9. Ask the student to find a comfortable position in the chair or on the ball. Invite him to feel his feet touching the floor, the support of what he is sitting on and his breath as he inhales and exhales. Make sure that he feels grounded, centered and safe.

10. Begin the sensation work as soon as the child is ready. First have him describe a sensation of something that brings comfort or pleasure. If he hasn't had any resourceful feelings since the event, have him choose a time before the event when he had good feelings and describe what he feels like now as he recalls those good feelings.

11. The child might automatically describe symptoms, or you may need to ask what kinds of difficulties he is struggling with since the event. Then ask him to describe what he is feeling. The following are sample questions and comments to use as a guide for inviting awareness of sensations:

    a. As you see the picture in your mind of "the man behind the tree" [for example], what do you notice in your body?

    b. And when you worry that he might come back, what do you notice in your body?

    c. And when you feel your tummy getting tight, what else do you notice? Tight like what? What might it look like? Can you show me where you feel it?

    d. And when you look at the rock . . . or make the rock with your fist . . . what happens next?

    e. And when you feel your legs shaking, what do you suppose your legs might want to do?

    f. When your legs feel like running, imagine that you are running in your favorite place and your [insert the name of a favorite safe person] will be waiting for you when you arrive.

    g. Or, have the child imagine running like his favorite animal. Encourage him to feel the power in his legs as he moves quickly with the wind on his face.

12. The idea is to follow the student's lead. Help him to explore, with an attitude of curiosity, what happens next as he notices his internal responses.

Note: please refer to Chapter II for detailed information on emotional first aid for coming out of shock. If loved ones have died, see Chapter VII to help children with the grieving process. For more activities and ideas for parents, teachers and counselors to use at school, please refer to *Trauma Through A Child's Eyes*, Chapter Eleven.

As we said in the beginning of the book, trauma is a fact of life. No one grows up without encountering at least some of this monster. But the good news is that trauma doesn't have to be a life sentence. With the simple tools you have learned to support your child's innate resilience, parents can be reassured that they can promote confidence and joy in their kids. And in this way *you* can change the world, one child at a time—and, if so inspired, one institution at a time. Thank you, committed parents, for making the effort to learn about these tools. Your children are our hope for the future.

Notes

CHAPTER I

1. Peter A. Levine, *Waking the Tiger: Healing Trauma* (Berkeley, CA: North Atlantic Books, 1997).
2. Ibid.
3. Antonio R. Damasio, *The Feeling of What Happens: Body and Emotion in the Making of Consciousness* (New York: Harcourt, Inc., 1999).

CHAPTER II

1. Joseph E. LeDoux, *The Emotional Brain: Mysterious Underpinnings of Emotional Life* (New York: Simon and Schuster, 1998).
2. Robert Fulford, DO, personal communication, Summer session, New England College of Osteopathic Medicine, Biddeford, Maine, 1980.

CHAPTER III

1. Lenore Terr, MD, *Too Scared To Cry: Psychic Trauma in Childhood* (New York: Basic Books, A Division of Harper Collins Publishers, 1990), p. 235.
2. C.G. Jung, *Structure and Dynamics of the Psyche, Collected Works, Vol. 8,* second edition (Princeton, NJ: Princeton University Press, 1969).
3. Violet Oaklander, *Hidden Treasures: A Map to the Child's Inner Self* (London: Karnac Books, 2006), pp. 32–33.
4. "The Magic in Me" poem was written by Maggie Kline and Peter Levine and excerpted from: Peter A. Levine, *It Won't Hurt Forever: Guiding Your Child Through Trauma* (Audio Learning Program) (Boulder, CO: Sounds True, 2001). Contact www.soundstrue.com or call (800) 333-9185.

CHAPTER IV

1. Robert Fulford, DO, personal communication, Summer session, New England College of Osteopathic Medicine, Biddeford, Maine, 1980.
2. Judith Acosta, LCSW, and Simon Prager, PhD, *The Worst Is Over: What to Say When Every Moment Counts (Verbal First Aid to Calm, Relieve Pain, Promote Healing and Save Lives)* (San Diego, CA: Jodere Group, 2002).
3. D. M. Levy, "On the problem of movement restraints," *American Journal of Orthopsychiatry,* Vol. 14: p. 644 (1944).

4. Susan Brink, "Soothing the Littlest Patients: Doctors Focus on Easing Pain in Kids," *U.S. News & World Report,* June 12, 2000. www.usnews.com.

5. K. Yashpal, J. Katz, and T.J. Coderre. "Effects of Preemptive or Post-Injury Intrathecal Local Anesthesia on Persistent Nociceptive Responses." *Anesthesiology* (1996).

   C. Michaloliakou, F. Chung, S. Sharma, "Preoperative Multimodal Analgesia Facilitates Recovery after Ambulatory Laparoscopic Cholecystectomy," *Anesth. Analg.* (1996).

   S. I. Marshall and F. Chung, "Discharge Criteria and Complications After Ambulatory Surgery," *Anesth. Analg.* Vol. 88, No. 3: p. 508 (March 1, 1999).

6. Peter Levine, personal communication in interviews with both sets of parents.

7. Brink, 2000.

8. Ibid. (From a 1998 study in the *Archives of Pediatrics & Adolescent Medicine*).

CHAPTER V (No notes)

CHAPTER VI

1. Alfred Kinsey et al., *Sexual Behavior of the Human Female* (Philadelphia: W.B. Saunders, 1953).

2. Children's Hospital National Medical Center, Washington, DC (www.safechild.org), 2006.

3. Harborview Medical Center, Harborview Center for Sexual Assault and Traumatic Stress (Seattle, WA, 2006). www.depts.washington.edu/hcsats/pdf/factsheets/csafacts.pdf.

   National Committee for Prevention of Child Abuse, "Basic Facts About Sexual Child Abuse."

   The following statistics are from the National Incident-Based Reporting System (NIBRS):

   > Sixty-seven percent of all victims of sexual assault reported to law enforcement agencies were juveniles (under the age of 18); 34% of all victims were under age 12.

   > One of every seven victims of sexual assault reported to law enforcement agencies was under age 6.

   > 40% of the offenders who victimized children under age 6 were juveniles (under the age of 18).

   > The data are based on reports from law enforcement agencies of twelve states and include the years 1991 through 1996. (Bureau of Justice Statistics www.ojp.usdoj.gov/bjs/, 2006)

4. Groth, 1982; DeFrancis, 1969; Russell, 1983. As reported by the Children's Hospital National Medical Center, Washington, DC (www.safechild.org), 2006.

5. Caren Adams and Jennifer Fay, *No More Secrets: Protecting Your Child from Sexual Assault* (San Luis Obispo, CA: Impact Publishers, 1984).

6. Vernon R. Wiehe, *Sibling Abuse: Hidden Physical, Emotional, and Sexual Trauma* (Thousand Oaks, CA: Sage Publications, 1997), p. 59.

7. *Child Adolescent Psychiatry Journal*, Vol. 35: 1 (January 1996); Criminal Justice Source Statistics (2000, Table 4.7, p. 362).

8. J.V. Becker and E.M. Coleman, *Handbook of Family Violence* (New York: Plenum Press, 1988), pp. 197–205.

9. Caren Adams and Jennifer Fay, *No More Secrets*.

10. Marilyn Van Derbur, *Miss America By Day: Lessons Learned from Ultimate Betrayals and Unconditional Love* (Denver, CO: Oak Hill Ridge Press, 2003).

11. Jan Hindman, *Just Before Dawn: From the Shadows of Tradition to New Reflections in Trauma Assessment and Treatment of Sexual Victimization* (Lincoln City, OR: AlexAndria Associates, 1989), p. 87.

12. Jennifer Freyd, *Betrayal Trauma* (Cambridge: Harvard University Press, 1996), p. 190.

Suggested listening (audio program) for this chapter: Peter A. Levine, *Sexual Healing: Transforming the Sacred Wound* (Louisville, CO: Sounds True, 2003).

CHAPTER VII

1. William Steele and Melvyn Raider, *Structured Sensory Intervention for Traumatized Children, Adolescents and Parents*, Volume I of the Mellen Studies in Social Work Series (United Kingdom: Edwin Mellen Press, Ltd., 2001), p. 155.

2. Judith S. Wallerstein, Julia M. Lewis and Sandra Blakeslee, *The Unexpected Legacy of Divorce: A 25-Year Landmark Study* (New York: Hyperion, 2000). A debate between Dr. E. Mavis Hetherington (who co-authored the book listed below in note 3) and Dr. Judith Wallerstein (who conducted studies reported in *The Unexpected Legacy of Divorce*) was reported on by Mary Duenwald in *The New York Times*, March 26, 2002.

3. Dr. E. Mavis Hetherington and John Kelly, *For Better or Worse: Divorce Reconsidered* (New York: W.W. Norton & Company, Inc., 2002).

4. Vicki Lansky, "Divorce: 10 Things I Learned" (Oxygen Media, 2001). www.oxygen.com/topic/family/fammtrs/divorce10_20011109.html.

5. Judith S. Wallerstein, Julia M. Lewis, and Sandra Blakeslee, *The Unexpected Legacy of Divorce*, p. 216.

C.M. Heinke and I. Westheimer, *Brief Separations* (New York: International University Press, 1965).

J. Soloman and C. George, "The Development of Attachment in Separated and Divorced Families: Effects of Overnight Visitation, Parent and Couple Variables," *Attachment and Human Development*, Vol. I, No. 1: 2–33 (April 1999).

6. E. Mavis Hetherington, "An Overview of the Virginia Longitudinal Study of Divorce and Remarriage with a Focus on Early Adolescence," *Journal of Family Psychology*, Vol. 7, No. 1: 39–56 (June 1993).

7. Elizabeth Kübler-Ross, *On Death and Dying* (New York: Macmillan, 1969).

8. John W. James and Russell Friedman, *When Children Grieve* (New York: Harper Collins, 2001).

   The Grief Recovery Institute, www.grief-recovery.com

   In U.S., contact P.O. Box 6061-382, Sherman Oaks, CA 91413. Telephone: (818) 907-9600.

   In Canada, contact RR#1, St. Williams, Ontario, Canada N0E 1P0. Telephone: (519) 586-8825.

CHAPTER VIII

1. Adapted and inspired by the spirit of John Lennon from "Revolution" on his *Imagine* album.

2. Phone interview conducted on July 14, 2006. Karen Schanche, MSW, LCSW, is a clinical social worker/psychotherapist who works as part of three multi-disciplinary teams at the University of California at San Francisco Medical Center: the Pediatric Rheumatology and Rehabilitation Medicine teams, and the Cancer Center's Symptom Management and Palliative Care Outpatient Service at the Comprehensive Cancer Center of UCSF. She can be reached at (415) 455-4915 or via email: karen.schanche@ucsfmedctr.org; or kschanche@earthlink.net.

3. Make-A-Wish Foundation is a national organization with a different website and address for each state. The main web address is: www.wish.org to locate their affiliates in each state.

4. K. Yashpal, J. Katz, and T.J. Coderre, "Effects of preemptive or post-injury intrathecal local anesthesia on persistent nociceptive responses," *Anesthesiology* (1996).

   C. Michaloliakou, F. Chung, and S. Sharma, "Preoperative multimodal analgesia facilitates recovery after ambulatory laparoscopic cholecystectomy," *Anesth. Analg.* (1996).

   S. I. Marshall and F. Chung, "Discharge Criteria and Complications After Ambulatory Surgery," *Anesth. Analg.*, Vol. 88, No. 3: 508 (March 1, 1999).

5. Interview with Maggie Kline, July 25, 2006. Contact this organization at: National Mass Fatalities Institute, Lisa R. LaDue, MSW, LISW, Kirkwood Community College, 6301 Kirkwood Blvd. SW, Cedar Rapids, IA 52404. Telephone: (319) 398-7122.

Bibliography

Acosta, Judith, LCSW, and Simon Prager, PhD. *The Worst Is Over: What to Say When Every Moment Counts (Verbal First Aid to Calm, Relieve Pain, Promote Healing and Save Lives)*. San Diego, CA: Jodere Group, 2002.

Adams, Caren, and Jennifer Fay. *No More Secrets: Protecting Your Child from Sexual Assault*. San Luis Obispo, CA: Impact Publishers, 1984.

Ames, Louise Bates, Clyde Gillespie, Jacqueline Haines, and Frances Ilg. *The Gesell Institute's Child Development from One to Six*. New York: Harper & Row, 1979.

Arms, Suzanne. *Immaculate Deception II*. Berkeley, CA: Celestial Arts, 1994.

Baker, Dr. Leigh. *Protecting Your Children From Sexual Predators*. New York: St. Martin's Press, 2002.

Bowlby, J. *A Secure Base: Parent-Child Attachment and Healthy Human Development*. New York: Basic Books, 2000.

Bowlby, J. *Separation: Anxiety and Anger*. New York: Basic Books, 2000.

Brazelton, T. Berry, MD. *Touchpoints: The Essential Reference, Your Child's Emotional and Behavioral Development*. United States: Addison-Wesley, 1992.

Brink, Susan. "Soothing the Littlest Patients: Doctors Focus on Easing Pain in Kids." *U.S. News & World Report*, June 12, 2000. www.usnews.com.

Damasio, Antonio R. *Descartes' Error: Emotion, Reason, and the Human Brain*. New York: Harper Perennial, 1995.

Damasio, Antonio R. *The Feeling of What Happens: Body and Emotion in the Making of Consciousness*. New York: Harcourt, Inc., 1999.

Freyd, Jennifer. *Betrayal Trauma*. Cambridge: Harvard University Press, 1996.

Henderson, Julie. *Embodying Well-Being or How to Feel as Good as You Can in Spite of Everything*. Napa, CA: Zapchen, 1999.

Herman, Judith Lewis, MD. *Trauma and Recovery*. New York: Basic Books, 1992.

Hetherington, E. Mavis. "An Overview of the Virginia Longitudinal Study of Divorce and Remarriage with a Focus on Early Adolescence." *Journal of Family Psychology* 7, no. 1 (June 1993): 39–56.

Hetherington, E. Mavis, and John Kelly. *For Better or Worse: Divorce Reconsidered.* New York: Norton, 2002.

James, John W., and Russell Friedman. *When Children Grieve.* New York: Harper Collins, 2001.

Karr-Morse, Robin, and Meredith W. Wiley. *Ghosts from the Nursery: Tracing the Roots of Violence.* New York: The Atlantic Monthly Press, 1997.

Kohut, Heinz. *The Restoration of the Self.* New York: International University Press, 1977.

Kübler-Ross, Elizabeth. *On Death and Dying.* New York: Macmillan, 1969.

LeDoux, Joseph E. *The Emotional Brain: Mysterious Underpinnings of Emotional Life.* New York: Simon and Schuster, 1998.

Leo, Pam. *Connection Parenting: Parenting Through Connection Instead of Coercion.* Deadwood, OR: Wyatt-MacKenzie Publishing, Inc., 2005.

Levine, Peter, and Maggie Kline. *Trauma Through A Child's Eyes: Awakening the Ordinary Miracle of Healing.* Berkeley, CA: North Atlantic Books, 2007.

Levine, Peter. *Healing Trauma: A Pioneering Program for Restoring the Wisdom of Your Body* (a book and CD); *It Won't Hurt Forever: Guiding Your Child Through Trauma;* and *Sexual Healing: Transforming the Sacred Woun,* (the latter two are primarily audio programs). All available from Sounds True, Louisville, CO.

Levine, Peter. *Waking the Tiger: Healing Trauma.* Berkeley, CA: North Atlantic Books, 1997.

Levy, D.M. "On the problem of movement restraints," *American Journal of Orthopsychiatry,* Vol. 14: 644 (1944).

Marshall, James. *George and Martha.* New York: Houghton Mifflin Co., 1972.

Marshall, S.I., and F. Chung, "Discharge Criteria and Complications After Ambulatory Surgery." *Anesth. Analg.* 88, no. 3 (March 1, 1999): 508.

McCarty, Wendy Anne, PhD. *Being with Babies: What Babies Are Teaching Us, An Introduction, 1.* Goleta, CA: Wondrous Beginnings, 1996. (Available through www.wondrousbeginnings.com.)

McCarty, W.A. *Being with Babies: What Babies Are Teaching Us, Supporting Babies' Innate Wisdom, 2.* Goleta, CA: Wondrous Beginnings, 1997. Available through www.wondrousbeginnings.com.

Michaloliakou, C., F. Chung, and S. Sharma. "Preoperative Multimodal Analgesia Facilitates Recovery After Ambulatory Laparoscopic Cholecystectomy." *Anesth Analg* (1996).

Montagu, Ashley. *Touching: The Human Significance of the Skin,* third edition. New York: Harper & Row, 1971.

Neufeld, Gordon, PhD, and Gabor Maté, MD. *Hold On To Your Kids: Why Parents Need to Matter More Than Peers.* Toronto, Ontario, Canada: Knopf, 2004.

Oaklander, Violet. *Hidden Treasures: A Map to the Child's Inner Self.* London, England: Karnac Books, 2006.

Oaklander, Violet. *Windows to Our Children.* Moab, UT: Real People Press, 1978.

Pearce, Joseph Chilton. *Evolution's End: Claiming the Potential of Our Intelligence.* New York: HarperCollins Publishers, 1992.

Pearce, Joseph Chilton. *Magical Child: Rediscovering Nature's Plan for Our Children.* New York: Dutton, 1977; reprinted by Penguin Books (Plume) in 1992.

Perry, Bruce. *Violence and Childhood: How Persisting Fear Can Alter the Developing Child's Brain.* The Child Trauma Academy, Department of Psychiatry and Behavioral Sciences, Baylor College of Medicine, Texas Children's Hospital, 1996.

Perry, Bruce D., MD, PhD. *The Vortex of Violence: How Children Adapt and Survive in a Violent World,* published online by the Child Trauma Academy, 2000. www.childtrauma.org.

Perry, Bruce D. "Incubated in Terror: Neurodevelopmental factors in the 'cycle of violence,'" in *Children, Youth and Violence: The Search for Solutions,* J. Osofsky, ed. New York: Guilford Press, 1997.

Perry, B.D., R. Pollard, T. Blakely, W. Baker, and D. Vigilante. "Childhood Trauma, the neurobiology of adaptation and 'use-dependent' development of the brain: how 'states' become 'traits'." *Infant Mental Health Journal,* Vol. 16, no. 4: 271–291 (1995).

Porges, Stephen W. "Neuroception: A Subconscious System for Detecting Threats and Safety." *Zero to Three Journal,* Vol. 24, no. 5: 19–24 (May 2004).

Rothenberg, Mira. *Children with Emerald Eyes: Histories of Extraordinary Boys and Girls.* Berkeley, CA: North Atlantic Books, 2003.

Sapolsky, Robert M. *Why Zebras Don't Get Ulcers: An Updated Guide to Stress, Stress Related Diseases, and Coping.* New York: W.H. Freeman & Company, 1994.

Scaer, Robert. *The Trauma Spectrum.* New York: Norton, 2005.

Schore, Allan N. *Affect Dysregulation and Disorders of the Self.* New York: W.W. Norton & Company, 2003.

Schore, Allan N. *Affect Regulation and the Origin of the Self: The Neurobiology of Emotional Development.* Hillsdale, NJ: Lawrence Erlbaum Associates, 1994.

Siegel, Daniel J., MD. *The Developing Mind: How Relationships and the Brain Interact to Shape Who We Are.* New York: The Guilford Press, 1999.

Siegel, Daniel J., MD, and Mary Hartzell, M.Ed. *Parenting from the Inside Out: How a Deeper Self-Understanding Can Help You Raise Children Who Thrive.* New York: Jeremy P. Tarcher/Penguin, 2003.

Soloman, J., and C. George. "The Development of Attachment in Separated and Divorced Families: Effects of Overnight Visitation, Parent and Couple Variables." *Attachment and Human Development I,* no. 1: 2–33 (April 1999).

Somé, Sobonfu E. *Welcoming Spirit Home: Ancient African Teachings to Celebrate Children and Community.* Novato, CA: New World Library, 1999.

Steele, William, and Melvyn Raider. *Structured Sensory Intervention for Traumatized Children, Adolescents and Parents,* Volume I of the Mellen Studies in Social Work Series. United Kingdom: Edwin Mellen Press, Ltd., 2001.

Stewart, John, PhD. *Beyond Time Out: A Practical Guide to Understanding and Serving Students with Behavioral Impairments in the Public Schools.* Gorham, ME: Hastings Clinical Associates, 2000.

Takikawa, Debby. Documentary DVD (narrated by Noah Wyle). *What Babies Want: An Exploration of the Consciousness of Infants* (2005). Contact Beginnings Inc., A Resource Center for Children and Families, P.O. Box 681, Los Olivos, CA 93441. Telephone: (800) 893-5070; www.what babieswant.com.

Terr, Lenore, MD. *Too Scared To Cry: Psychic Trauma in Childhood.* New York: Basic Books, A Division of Harper Collins Publishers, 1990.

Van Derbur, Marilyn. *Miss America By Day: Lessons Learned from Ultimate Betrayals and Unconditional Love.* Denver, CO: Oak Hill Ridge Press, 2003.

van der Kolk, Bessel A., Alexander C. McFarlane, and Lars Weisaeth, eds. *Traumatic Stress: The Effects of Overwhelming Experience on Mind, Body, and Society.* New York: The Guilford Press, 1996.

Wallerstein, Judith S., Julia M. Lewis, and Sandra Blakeslee. *The Unexpected Legacy of Divorce: A 25-Year Landmark Study.* New York: Hyperion, 2000.

Wiehe, Vernon R. *Sibling Abuse: Hidden Physical, Emotional, and Sexual Trauma.* Thousand Oaks, CA: Sage Publications, 1997.

Yashpal, K., J. Katz, and T.J. Coderre. "Effects of Preemptive or Post-Injury Intrathecal Local Anesthesia on Persistent Nociceptive Responses." *Anesthesiology* (1996).

Zand, Walton, and Roundtree. *A Parents' Guide to Medical Emergencies: First Aid for Your Child.* Avery Publishing Group, 1997.

Additional Resources

Alliance for Transforming the Lives of Children. This is an evidence-based source of information for parents on consciously conceiving, birthing and nurturing children at www.atlc.org.

Balametrics offers equipment such as balance boards and sensory integration tools for educators, parents and therapists. Visit their website at www.balametrics.com or call (800) 894-3187 or (360) 452-2842. To write: Balametrics, Inc., P.O. Box 2716, Port Angeles, WA 98362, or email: info@balametrics.com.

BEBA (Building and Enhancing Bonding and Attachment): A Center for Family Healing, Santa Barbara, CA. Specializing in early infant trauma and family therapy, through publications, conference presentations, video and parent education groups. Website: www.beba.org.

Birthing The Future, P.O. Box 1040, Bayfield, CO 81122. Telephone: (970) 884-4090. This is a non-profit organization to support the child-bearing woman and share the finest world wisdom about ancient, traditional and contemporary childbirth beliefs and practices. Information and products can be found at www.Birthing TheFuture.com.

Calm Birth, a Childbirth Method for the 21st Century. See www. CalmBirth.org or email to info@CalmBirth.org. The practices transform the birth process and imprint a peaceful beginning on both mother and child.

www.childbirthconnection.org (an evidence-based maternity care non-profit organization).

Elora Media: Children's books, videos and music to enrich creativity. Website: www.eloramedia.com.

Foundation for Human Enrichment. 6685 Gunpark Dr., Boulder, Colorado, Telephone: (303) 652-4035; Fax: (303) 652- 4039. The FHE, founded by Dr. Peter A. Levine, is a non-profit, educational and research organization dedicated to the worldwide healing and prevention of trauma. Professional training in Somatic Experiencing® is provided, as well as outreach to underserved populations. www.traumahealing.com.

International Trauma-Healing Institute (ITI), 269 South Lorraine Blvd., Los Angeles, CA 90004. Contact Gina Ross, Founder and President of ITI, at www.traumainstitute.org, for trauma outreach, prevention and healing in the Middle East and worldwide.

Lisa R. LaDue, MSW, LISW, Senior Advisor (Co-founder and former Director), National Mass Fatalities Institute, Kirkwood Community College, 6301 Kirkwood Blvd. SW, Cedar Rapids, IA 52404. Telephone: (319) 398-7122. Website: www.nmfi.org.

Peter A. Levine, *Healing Trauma: A Pioneering Program for Restoring the Wisdom of Your Body,* book and CD published by Sounds True, Louisville, CO, 2005.

    Peter A. Levine, *It Won't Hurt Forever: Guiding Your Child through Trauma,* CD published by Sounds True, Louisville, CO, 2001.

    Peter A. Levine, *Sexual Healing: Transforming the Sacred Wound,* CD published by Sounds True, Louisville, CO, 2003.

Dr. Belleruth Naparstek, *Successful Surgery,* an imagery CD to prepare for medical procedures; available from www.healthy journeys.com.

TOUCHPOINTS, Ed Tronick, 1295 Boylston, Suite 320, Boston, MA 02115. Telephone: (617) 355-5913. Early education for professionals in emotional and behavioral areas.

Trauma Outreach Program (TOP) is an FHE program that serves victims of trauma through outreach, education, training and research throughout the world. It was created post-tsunami in 2005 in Thailand. Website: www.traumahealing.com.

Trauma Vidya was created in India after the Indian Ocean tsunami of 2004 and to provide relief to those in India suffering from symptoms of traumatic stress through education, training, treatment and research. Contact: Raja Selvam, Founder, at www.trauma vidya.org.

About the Authors

Peter A. Levine, PhD, has been a pioneer in the field of trauma for nearly forty years. He is the developer of Somatic Experiencing® and founder of the Colorado-based Foundation for Human Enrichment, which is dedicated to the dissemination of his original, creative work. Dr. Levine was a stress consultant for NASA on the development of the space shuttle project and served on the American Psychological Association's Presidential Initiative on Responding to Large-Scale Disasters and Ethno-Political Warfare. His current interests include making his work available to underserved populations. Dr. Levine is the author of the best-selling book *Waking the Tiger: Healing Trauma* (North Atlantic Books), available in twenty languages, and the book/CD *Healing Trauma: A Pioneering Program for Restoring the Wisdom of Your Body* (Sounds True) as well as the audio learning series *It Won't Hurt Forever: Guiding your Child through Trauma* and *Sexual Healing: Transforming the Sacred Wound.*

Maggie Kline, a retired school psychologist, has been a marriage, family and child therapist in Long Beach, California, for almost twenty-five years. Integrating Somatic Experiencing® with dream work, art and play therapy, she works extensively with individuals, couples, teens and children to prevent and heal trauma and stress-related disorders. Kline, a senior Somatic Experiencing® instructor, teaches Dr. Levine's method to professionals and at specially-designed workshops in the U.S. and Europe that help educators help kids. She also worked with groups of kids in the FHE-sponsored trauma relief effort in Thailand following the 2004

Indian Ocean tsunami. Before becoming a psychologist, Kline was a master teacher for Long Beach Unified School District, a school counselor and a parent. Her rich and varied background in working with children from diverse cultures and of all ages, from preschool through high school, brings clarity to the practical steps outlined in this book. Kline is the co-author, with Dr. Levine, of "It Won't Hurt Forever: Guiding Your Child Through Trauma" (*Mothering* magazine) and *Trauma Through A Child's Eyes: Awakening the Ordinary Miracle of Healing* (North Atlantic Books).

Foundation for Human Enrichment

The FHE is a nonprofit, educational and research organization dedicated to the worldwide healing and prevention of trauma. It offers professional training in Somatic Experiencing® a short-term naturalistic approach to the resolution and healing of trauma developed by Dr. Levine. It also provides outreach to underserved populations and victims of violence, war and natural disasters.

Contact us for further information at:

Foundation for Human Enrichment
6685 Gunpark Dr., Suite 102
Boulder, Colorado 80301
Telephone: (303) 652-4035
Fax: (303) 652-4039
www.traumahealing.com

About North Atlantic Books

North Atlantic Books (NAB) is a 501(c)(3) nonprofit publisher committed to a bold exploration of the relationships between mind, body, spirit, culture, and nature. Founded in 1974, NAB aims to nurture a holistic view of the arts, sciences, humanities, and healing. To make a donation or to learn more about our books, authors, events, and newsletter, please visit www.northatlanticbooks.com.